Lost No More

a memoir

by CeeCee James

Prologue

Everyone has a story. You may have read mine, in Ghost No More. Now, it's my honor to share my beloved's. This book is dedicated to him, and my thankfulness that our stories merged.

Lost No More is based on true events, memories shared with me through the years by my husband, and a few brain storming nights where I interviewed him like crazy. Jim read it as I wrote, telling me what I needed to reword to give the most accurate portrayal of his life. Only the names and places have been changed out of respect for the people in the memoir.

I did my best to reveal the true flavor of his life as he journeyed towards love. It's a journey we're all on. And, if you haven't heard it recently, then let me tell you that you are worth your journey.

Chapter 1

"Get my mitt, Jimmy," Dad yelled, his face pulled into a cocky grin. He tugged his red shirt down, then pulled the crease straight on his white pants.

"Where is it, Dad?" I sat on the stairs watching him.

"You're four, you're a big boy now. Go find it."

I jumped up and darted down the hall to the living room, spotting the well-worn glove on the buffet on the way. After scooping it up, I ran it over to him.

He took it from my hand and tried it on, giving the creased palm a punch. "Thanks."

I wanted him to ruffle my hair. Instead he looked in the mirror and pulled his cap low on his brow.

Then he yelled "Goodbye, Pearl," and left me standing in the open doorway as he strutted towards his truck. At the truck door he looked back at me and winked. "See you later, alligator."

I wiggled inside and answered back, "After a while, crocodile."

I used to think he was famous. But then I found out the monogrammed "M" on his shirt stood for the local bar.

Later, that afternoon, Mom packed me and my baby brother, David, up in the car and drove us down to Union Parkway. We reached the hot metal bleachers just as Dad swaggered up to the home plate. He gave a wolf whistle to the pitcher, who squinted at him and tried to sneer. Dad laughed. His confidence made me swell with pride. Dad tapped the plate and gave his twisted smile.

The pitcher spit in his hand then wound up and let a curve ball fly.

Crack!

Dad smacked it past the outfielders like a rocket. My seat shook under me as the crowd jumped to their feet and screamed.

I skipped off the bleachers and ran down to the chain fence. My fingers looped through the metal links as I pressed my face against it and shouted. "Go Dad! Go!" His cleats pounded up the dust as the ball chased him from base to base. My chest almost blew apart as he slid into home plate in a cloud of dirt.

"Yeah! That's my Dad!"

They won 3-2.

After the game, Dad didn't look over at me. Instead, he rushed to his teammates and they jumped about and hugged each other. I smiled to see him laughing so hard.

Dad hung around after the game and didn't come home with the rest of us. As Mom made dinner I overheard her say to herself, "He's going to come home a stumbling idiot," with worried lines on her face.

After we finished eating and had bath-time, I sat in a waste-paper basket in front of the TV. The plastic cupped my back while my legs, in dinosaur pajamas, hung over the edge. The living room was dark, but cozy, with a little light coming from the hanging kitchen lamp. The kids on the television jumped in the air. I beat my hands against the sides of the can and sang along. "Doo, do, do, do!"

Mom was washing dishes in the kitchen when the back door crashed open. I flinched. Dad walked into the kitchen with big, stomping steps. I heard a pan slam, then loud voices.

If I'm quiet and pretend I'm not here, they won't notice me. Staring hard at the TV, I tried to concentrate on what the green puppet on the screen was saying. Bits of my parents' words broke through my focus, as though the puppet were speaking their words.

"You're drunk! Like always!"

"I had good reason to celebrate!"

"Celebrate what? A bar win?"

"I'm sick of your nagging, Woman!"

A loud clatter rang out as a dish fell in the sink.

And then another.

I didn't dare turn around. My bottom lip trembled. I took a deep breath. "I'm not here, you don't see me," I repeated over and over and concentrated on the TV.

There was prickly silence.

Then, a metallic clang and the light dimmed as Mom screamed.

A gust of wind blew past me just before the TV exploded in bright light. I jerked back and toppled over out of the basket.

The TV hissed with a flicker of sparks.

Inside the broken screen, the ceiling light rocked to a stop. Dad had thrown the fixture with the speed of a fast ball at the TV.

My world spun around me with shock, and I felt a wave of nausea. He's mad at me! Why is he mad at me? What did I do wrong?

Dad stomped into the living room. I shrank away from him.

"Just look what you made me do!" His eyes and hair were wild as he wrenched the fixture out of the TV. I didn't know who he was talking to. He swung the light to one side, where it rolled into the couch, fumbled for his keys, and stormed out the front door.

*****

The next day Dad looked at the broken TV with a bemused expression.

"Don't you remember what happened?" Mom asked.

"No, I really don't," he said with a shrug. "I'll call Larry. He'll be able to repair that. I've seen him take an entire set apart and put it back together." He turned to me. "One handed! With his eyes closed!"

I grinned.

The phone rang, and Mom walked over to the table to answer it. She sounded cheery, and her head nodded, as though the speaker on the other end could see. After hanging up, her happy look faded away. "That was Ralph." She looked at Dad sharply. "You didn't tell me there's a get together today."

"Well, we've got to celebrate our win!" Dad rubbed his hands together and then patted his pocket looking for his cigarettes.

"But aren't we going to church?"

"Aww, why do I need to go, Pearl? I live by my motto; Look up." He pointed towards the ceiling.

"I seem to remember you did your celebrating last night." Mom unbuckled the baby from the yellow bouncy seat sitting on the floor. She handed him to Dad. "You'd do better to spend more time looking up than looking at your drink."

"What?" he said, patting my brother on the back. "I already said I was sorry. I ain't going to drink today."

I crossed my fingers and toes, hoping it would be that way.

We piled in the car, and Dad drove us to Big Bend River Park. He turned into the dirt lot and pulled in next to his friend's truck. The car had hardly come to a complete stop before Dad leapt out to help his friend carry an ice-chest across the grounds to the burn pit.

Mom watched him leave, two angry lines appearing between her eyebrows. She sighed as she struggled to get the baby out of the car seat. I followed her, looping the heavy diaper bag across my shoulder. She wandered over the grass to the trees that edged the park until she found a flat spot in the shade.

"This is good," she said. I dumped the bag and ran to find Dad.

"Get me a soda!" she called after me.

He was standing by the smoking BBQ surrounded by a mob of people. I could hardly get close to him with everyone crowded around. They slapped his back and laughed at his jokes. Someone passed him a bottle of beer.

I remembered Mom's soda and grabbed one out of the ice-chest. Mom had spread a towel and rested, propped on her arms. My baby brother slept in a bundle next to her. Other moms had joined her with their own towels and babies.

Mom took the soda from my hand and asked, "Have you eaten yet? You be sure to eat something, Jimmy."

I nodded. After grabbing a hotdog burned black from the grill I tried to weasel in through the group of men to get close to Dad so he'd notice me. His dark eyes snapped as he yelled out the punchline to a joke I didn't understand. The men all laughed, bumping into me. I took a few steps back and shoved the end of the hotdog in my mouth.

The men's conversation changed to the Summer Day parade and the float that Maverick's Tavern was building for its champion baseball team. That meant Dad would be on it, and a bubble of excitement squirmed inside my chest. The whole town would see him, and know what a great baseball player he was. I thought about the neighbor kid, Logan, whose dad worked at the grocery store every day wearing a brown apron. Logan made fun of me because Dad had lost his job. Logan would see what a great man Dad was.

We were there until after dusk. The moon was coming up fat and bright over the mountain, and nearly everyone had already packed up and left the picnic. Just Dad and Jared were left by the fire drinking their last beer. Rocking the sleeping baby, Mom convinced Dad it was time to go.

We weren't home but a few minutes when I heard the hiss of Dad opening another beer. Mom froze for a moment before hustling me to my room. She put baby David in the crib across from my bed and fiddled with his blanket. Then she went to the drawer and brought out my favorite pajamas, the ones that had the spaceships all over them. I pulled them on and climbed into bed. She leaned down and tucked my blanket up to my chin.

"Goodnight Jim." She smiled at me before she kissed my forehead.

She shut the door, but it hardly muffled her words to him. Angry words. He snapped back; Mom's high droning interrupted by his sharp barks. There was a loud crash, and Mom yelled "Maybe you want to pull the cabinets down like you did the last time you were drunk?"

Dad shouted, "Will you just shut up?"

The front door slammed and, outside my window, Dad's truck roared to life. I heard Mom sigh, and the soft noises of her cleaning up the mess. I rolled over in bed to watch my baby brother in his crib. His arm stretched across his face and his lip wiggled like when he was hungry. He never woke, no matter how loud they fought. I wrapped my blanket around me. My eyes burned, but I was four. I was too big to cry.

*****

Finally the day of the parade arrived. Grandma, Mom, and I hauled out our lawn chairs from the back of the car and dragged them to the road. I jumped up and down, knocking into people surrounding me.

"Sit still, Jimmy!" Mom insisted.

I tried, but the tapping of my feet against the ground bothered her, too. "Fine, get up and jump then," she said with an eye roll.

The streets were lined with people. About a quarter of the way down the block I saw Logan. He sat with his parents, his hair sharply parted and slicked to the side, with black rimmed glasses on his skinny nose just like his dad. They both turned and looked at me, wearing identical sweater vests. Logan doesn't know what a cool Dad is. I snorted and looked away.

Just then I heard the fire trucks. Every year, they started the parade with their lights flashing and horns whooping. I whooped too as one of the firemen threw some wax lips my way, then sprinted to get them, nearly getting knocked over by a bigger kid. I crammed them in my mouth, feeling my teeth dig into the wax. The cherry vampire teeth hid my grin.

Confetti showered the air as the town's unicycle squad went by. Cheerleaders, rah-rahing with their pom-poms, clowns twisted sommer-saults on both sides of the Big Tex Restaurant float, and 4-H horses were followed by a man with a shovel and wheel barrel.

A banner held by two teenagers announced the High School marching band. Teens in white boots marched with high steps and pounded on drums. Cymbals clanged. One red-spotted boy tried to hang on to his hat while blowing into a tuba. I watched, fascinated, as the hat slipped side-ways held on only by the chin strap, the boy's eyes bulging from both embarrassment and effort.

We whistled and cheered. Then Mom called, "There they are." I spun around to look. My heart deflated a little when I saw the worn flat-bed trailer that was hauled by a busted up truck. There were a few limp blue streamers taped to a construction paper sign. In scraggly hand-drawn letters it said, "Mavericks, Home of the Boot-filled Beer."

Dad was front and center on a hay bale. With his best grin on his face he waved to the crowd, a cigarette dangling from his lip. I jumped up and down as the excitement roared in my chest, "Look, town! Look, Logan! That's my Dad!"

By Dad's foot was a dented bullhorn speaker. When his eyes caught mine he pulled the bullhorn to his mouth. I waved even harder. He notices me! He's going to say something!

Dad pointed at me and yelled out, "Jimmy likes to dance with a hole in his pants."

I stopped jumping. My face blushed red to the roots of my hair. I did not like to dance, and I never had holes in my pants. Mom made sure of that. Everyone turned to see who he was pointing at. There was laughter all around me. I grinned sheepishly and sat down.

Chapter 2

Sunday afternoon was chore day. With a bucket full of soap bubbles, I staggered away from the spigot and out to the front yard. I was only half-way there and already my arms ached.

Dad waited in the driveway, wearing cut-off jeans trimmed so short the pockets hung out the bottom. He sprayed down his green Dodge Dart, catching a rainbow in the water droplets.

Dad loved that car. Wherever we went, he'd park it in the back end of parking lots away from people. Last week, a blue El Camino pulled in next to the Dart, just before Dad and I got out. He opened his car door wide and smacked it into Dad's door. The stranger didn't say anything, just headed for the store.

Dad leapt out of the car. He ran his hands down the paint and then called after the guy, "Excuse me! You just dinged my door!"

I sat up a little straighter in my seat, a cold pit in my stomach. You don't mess with Dad.

The man spun back and shrugged his shoulders. "I wouldn't worry about that little mark."

Dad stared at the guy. He tapped a cigarette out of a pack from his front pocket, then lit a match with a snap and held it to the end. Took a long drag. Then grabbed the car door and slammed it again and again into the other guy's car.

Bam!

Bam!

The crashing rang through the parking lot. When he finished Dad eyeballed the man and said, "Well, I wouldn't worry about this mark either then."

The man's mouth dropped open. But he saw the look in Dad's eye and didn't move.

Dad climbed back into the Dart and the tires squealed as we squirreled out of the parking lot.

We turned on to the straight-away. Just before Dad hit the gas hard, he said, "Ready for this? Some heads are going to roll." I laughed as we got sucked back into our seats.

*****

In the fall of 1979 we moved out of the little house and up into a place tucked far back in the woods of Wildfire Rim. I was six. My little brother was four, a little snot-nosed kid who liked to follow me everywhere. At least that's what I told him. Truth is, he was my best friend.

Wildfire Rim was billed in the real estate brochures as a huge housing development, but the actual development was slow. In fact, all that had been built was a maze of dirt roads that swirled in and out of the green belt and led to nowhere. But, at the other end of the development was the queen mother of all fun places; a house nearly finished that begged to be explored.

David went to sneak a couple of sodas out of our fridge while I held watch. We jammed them in the pockets of our carpenter pants. Mom always dressed us the same way, and it was a drag, but what could you do?

"Good job getting 'em," I told David, then to cool him down, "But you forgot the granola bars."

He wrinkled his nose and scuffed his toe in the dirt.

"Aww that's okay. I'm not hungry anyway." I tousled his hair like I'd seen Dad do.

He gave me a smile and I hollered, "Let's go! Let's be like scouts!" That was our code word to be super stealthy. I ran down the side of the road with David hot on my heels, prepared to jump in the bushes and hide if anyone should drive up. We dove just in time as a big truck rumbled past with rafters bundled into giant triangles on its flat bed. We watched it go by with our noses in the dirt. Then we followed in spy mode. My belly scratched against the dead grass as I crawled to the edge of the half-built house.

The truck jerked to a stop and a construction guy in an orange vest directed the boom to lift the rafters off the bed. The rafters swayed in the air for a moment before the boom lowered them in the dirt yard of the house.

David elbowed me in the ribs and waggled his eyebrows in a crazy way at the rafters.

"I know!" I hissed. "Be quiet!"

After it was unloaded, the construction guys jumped back into the white truck, and, with the exhaust burping grey smoke, headed back down the dirt road.

David grinned at me, and we both dashed over the excavated yard to the rafters.

"Get on up there." I pointed.

He looked at my foot pinning down one end and scrambled up the other side. Slowly, I rose up in the air. We took turns walking towards the middle of the rafter, like a giant teeter totter, until we had enough weight at the top end and it would come slamming down. Then we ran to the other side to do it again.

After the third time it crashed down, I called out, "I'm done!" and jumped off just before he made it to the end, causing him to fall off.

"Hey! I'm telling!"

"Yeah, go tell Mom. She'll be real interested in knowing you're over here."

"Shut-up," he muttered, suddenly absorbed with a pile of putty on the ground. He kicked at it with his shoe.

"Scoot over. Let me see that." I scooped it up in my palm and rolled the blob into a ball. It started to stick with long strings to my hand.

David found another splotch of putty that sat in sawdust by some 2x4 board ends.

"Hey, be careful with it," I cautioned him, when he started to play with it. "This stuff'll stick to your clothes if you don't pay attention. Mom'll have a cow."

"Or your hair!" David added.

I snorted. At six, I knew to be careful not to get it in my hair.

I dropped the gooey ball, and dragged my hands through the dust in the yard that I hoped would one day be filled with neighbor kids to play with. Still wiping my hands together, I glanced over at the half-built house.

"Think there's a way in?" I examined the porch. No roof, but the front door looked bolted shut.

"Put that down and c'mon" I motioned to David. He dropped his blob and looked with big eyes at his gooey hands. I sighed.

"Wipe them there." I pointed to a soft pile of sawdust shavings, then walked over to the side of the house. The sun was at the horizon and streaks of orange came through the trees surrounding the cleared lot.

"Hurry up." I waved him along.

Down the side of the house were three windows, all with glass snug in their frames except for the last one, a gaping empty hole. I rushed over. "David! Check this out!"

He ran to me and stepped into my hands, my fingers looped like a stirrup. With a grunt, I hauled him up to the window edge, and he slithered through. I heaved myself up on my forearms on the window sill and squirmed through after him.

"Hello?" David yelled, then turned to flash me a gape-toothed grin at the echo. "Whoop! Whoop!" David scurried behind a lattice of boards of an unfinished wall.

"What do you think this room is?" I looked up at the wires hanging from the ceiling.

"Maybe a secret tunnel!"

"Don't be dumb, they don't build secret tunnels in new houses like this." Still, I hastily surveyed the floor for any possible signs of a trapdoor. "Hey check this out! Maybe it's some kind of safe."

We examined the metal box screwed into a beam. I opened the door; just a bunch of switches, then slammed it shut and walked down the hall.

David wouldn't walk in the hallway, and instead wove through each room through their skeleton walls. "Look! I'm a monkey escaping the zoo!" His hands gripped the boards as he squeezed his way between.

At the end of the hall stood the bare framework of a stairway. The workers had nailed a crooked handrail made of two by fours that traveled up its side. We looked at each other before racing up to the top.

"Don't push!"

"I'm telling Mom!"

All the rooms upstairs had been finished with white-board walls. The rough edge of the wall was cool like chalk, and I dug out a half moon dent from the plaster with my fingernail. Behind me David hummed. With a piece of plaster he'd written on the floor,

"Hi!" with a gargoyle smiley face. I sat next to him and added my own face, complete with sharp teeth. Bigger teeth than in his picture.

The light was getting darker. "Let's get out of here," I said. We hustled back down the stairs.

Outside, I found a bunch of black plastic ties that had held the rafters together. I dug through my pocket and pulled out a pack of matches that I'd snuck off our woodstove that morning when Mom wasn't looking.

"Jim! No! I'm gonna tell Mom!" David jumped up and down next to me, tugging my arm.

"Hush! Want to see something cool? Watch this." I lit the match with a quick snap like Dad always did and stared at the flame.

David's eyes were big, but he bent to watch as I cupped my hand around the spark. When the flame was strong, I held it to the end of one of the plastic ties. We watched the hot plastic burn and drip black dots onto the ground. It made a cool sound: Zip! Zip! Zip! Zip! David reached to touch one of the drops.

"Stop!" I hissed. "You don't want that on your skin."

I made a pile out of leaves, shavings and a few small branches, and held another match to the base. The flame made me think of the look on Dad's face when he yelled at the man. Tough. Strong.

"Yeah," I nodded. "I make my own rules." The dry kindling took right away, and I fed it a few more branches. Within minutes it was blazing into a nice bonfire. I looked around for something to cook, some old pinecone, or a left-over lunch from one of the workers.

Sitting by the steps of the house was a spray can.

"David," I pointed to the can. "Go bring me that."

"Why?"

"We're gonna put it in the fire. Dad says they explode when they get hot enough."

David looked unsure, but the promise of an explosion perked him up. He brought me the can, and I pushed it into the middle of the fire with a long stick. I covered it with more twigs and branches until it was a roaring pile. After a few minutes a pile of red embers cradled the can.

The can began to rock back and forth and started to tick.

"Uhh, David?"

"What?"

"Run!"

We both ran to the porch, and David scooted behind to use me as a shield.

The can exploded, blowing half the fire out in a shower of sparks. I poked my head up just in time to see what was left of the fire flaring along a greasy trail towards the house.

My heart beat into my throat.

"I told you Jim! I told you this would be bad!" David yelled.

"Dad's going to kill us!" I shouted, and ran over to stomp on the fire with my tennis shoes. Luckily, most of the wood had been scattered by the blast, and I was able to beat down the flames.

David trampled over the blackened ash for good measure when I was done.

"Wow!" David said, "The fire trucks might have come. And then you would have caught it!"

"Chill out, everything's fine," I answered. "You're probably going to tattle anyway."

"No," He rolled his eyes. "I don't tattle!"

I grinned at him. "That was pretty wicked."

We heard the train come rumbling along the tracks on its way up to the lake. It made two prolonged horn blasts as it crossed the main road.

"Crud! We're late!" I told David. It was dinner time and hopefully Dad would be home. If he wasn't, then he'd be coming home late smelling like alcohol, and there'd be fighting tonight.

When we ran through the back door, Dad was home. But he had a bucket of plaster, and was filling in a new fist size hole in the wall. Mom's lips were pressed into white lines while she stirred the macaroni noodles.

"You boys are late," Dad said and smoothed the plaster with a spackling knife.

"Don't you yell at my boys," Mom said.

Dad looked over at her and his shoulders tuck down. I swallowed and looked away. My heart felt heavy, not wanting to upset Mom for not taking her side, or disappoint Dad by seeing him get lectured by Mom.

David made a small noise, and his eyes looked watery. In that instant, I knew what to do. "Sorry we're late," I said to Dad. And, to David, "Come on. Let's go play Lincoln Logs in my room."

I didn't know what happened between my parents and the hole in the wall, and I didn't want to know. They looked ready to start up again. I just hoped the bedroom door would block out any arguing so David wouldn't hear.

Chapter 3

We were running late as usual, with only a half-hour until it was time for the church's harvest festival to start. Dad smeared green grease paint under my eyes, then grabbed my chin to turn my head. The paint felt heavy and wet on my face. He inspected it with a nod.

"There you go, you little fart. Now you look Army proud." He called my brother over to him as I climbed off the kitchen stool and ran to the bathroom to check it out.

"Did you do your face like this in the Army?" I yelled from the bathroom and stuck my tongue out at the mirror.

"Yeah, I'm sure I had it like that a time or two," Dad said, putting dark smears on David's face.

Every night this week, Dad had been coming home from his new job building docks on the lake with a smile on his face. There weren't any alcohol bottles clinking about in the back of his truck, and no boozy apologies for breaking things. He'd told Mom he quit drinking because life was good and alcohol would mess it up. "I've got this, Pearl."

Mom had said, "I hope so," and patted her belly. It was round with another baby.

Dad still got angry right quick, but it no longer had the crazy in it. Even so, I kept my guard up. I might be working with him on the car, both of us laughing and having a good time. Then, he'd need a tool, and maybe I wasn't holding the right one in my hand. All hell would break loose with his burst of swearing. The best defense was to freeze and let him rant, and not 'poke the bear', as Mom called it, in any way.

He put the last finishing touches on David's face, who then scrambled away to show Mom. She had his pirate costume ready and got my brother wiggling into it, while he called, "Where's my sword Ma?"

I buttoned my camo shirt and threw on a hunter's orange hat. Rounding the corner back to the living room, I winked at Mom and formed guns with my hands.

Dad said he was too tired to go tonight. "You kids have fun!" he said, and popped his recliner to watch Bonanza on TV.

We piled into Mom's rusty Datsun, and listened to the clutch grind as Mom tried to get it into gear. "Stupid car," Mom muttered, as she shifted again and again until it finally slipped into first. "Better," she smiled, and we drove to the party.

Outside the church were tall bundles of corn stalks and rows of orange pumpkins. My Sunday school teacher greeted me at the door dressed as a scare crow.

"Hi Mrs. Neely," I said to be polite because Mom was behind me.

"I'm not Mrs. Neely! I'm Scare-Crow." She smiled through a thick mask of face paint and scratched at her wrist where hay was stuffed in her flannel sleeve.

I rushed past her before I laughed and caught it from Mom.

There were hay bales and signs directing the crowds through the church. The gymnasium was an explosion of color and chaos where kids screeched, people laughed, and babies looked wide-eyed at the excitement. Thrumming inside of me was one thought, Candy! Candy! Candy!

I wasn't in the gymnasium two minutes when someone started to follow me disguised in a Batman costume.

"Hey! I know you!" He grabbed my arm, his eyes dark behind his black mask.

"Huh?"

"It's me, Logan!"

Oh great. Logan, the kid who wore matching sweater vests with his dad. "Hey," I answered, then pretended to be interested in a beanbag game on the other side of him.

"Can I have a turn?" I asked the clown the game. I grabbed the beanbags from her hand and took careful aim at the basket.

Another tug on my arm. Logan wasn't giving up.

"You know, I saw you the other day. We moved up to WildFire Rim, too. Yeah, you were playing outside with your brother."

I shrugged. Great, he's my neighbor again.

"Can we hang out sometime?" Logan asked.

I sighed inside, and reluctantly nodded. I couldn't be mean to his face. Besides, maybe he'd lost the sweater vest by now.

"Tomorrow maybe? By the horse pasture?"

I started to nod, when a refrigerator-sized box rammed into me and knocked me into Logan. I pushed off of Logan, and then shoved back at the box, annoyed. The cardboard was painted black, with crooked gold letters stenciled across the front that proclaimed "King James Bible." Blue jean legs stuck out from underneath. In between the "King" and "James" was a one inch slot cut into the cardboard.

I peered through the opening.

A water pistol materialized and shot a spray of water into my eyes. I jerked back while the box shook with silent laughter.

Wiping my eyes with my sleeve, I sneered, "Oh, you think you're so funny! Who are you anyway?"

Mom came up to my side. "Ohhh, who's in the box?" She gave a giggle and poked her fingers in the slot. "Hello in there." She peeked inside, and let out a shriek as the water hit her face. She back-tracked quickly, and staggered into to Pastor Larson for support.

Pastor Larson looked surprised by the sudden attack of a pregnant lady grabbing his shirt front, and let out a yelp. Mrs. Neely suddenly appeared asking Pastor Larson if he was okay. Together, they helped Mom get steady on her feet. Then, they all studied the bible.

It did a little sashay bow towards them and strode away through the crowd.

The bible walked around the party all night squirting unsuspecting people. Everyone laughed and tried to get a peek inside, before blinking sharply at the water in their eyes. I just itched to know who it was, and wished I'd thought of the idea myself.

When the party ended, Mom packed me and my brother into the car. David and I compared our treasures in the back seat.

"Hey! Look what I got. Want to trade?"

"Yuck! Black Jelly beans! No way!"

When we got home, Dad's car was in the driveway, but the house was dark. Mom flipped on the living room lights and threw her purse on the buffet, then let out a squeal.

There, in the middle of the floor, sat the large bible box.

Mom's mouth fell open.

"What the heck?" I trailed, off speechless. David ran over and climbed in the box and spun around, hollering, "Bam! Bam! Bam! I got you!"

Dad had pulled a good one over on us.

The next day Dad was as pleased as punch at the way he'd tricked every one. Mom wasn't so happy about it.

"Why'd you squirt me in the face, you, idiot?" She frowned at him while she slipped on her sneakers, heaving a breath over her big belly.

He just laughed as he grabbed his morning thermos, and headed out to work.

David and I slurped through our cereal as fast as we could. Mom picked off her apron from the back of the chair and unfolded it. She was about to leave for her job at the deli.

"You boys behave yourself today. Quit destroying the house. I have enough to do without coming home to this place looking like it's been chewed up and spit out."

David and I nodded. I scuffed my toe and looked down at the floor, trying to cough up a picture of innocence.

"Aww, that's my good boys," Mom said, and patted me on the head.

We listened to her car make its usual grinding noises until she pulled out of the driveway.

With big grins, David and I high-fived each other. We dove out the back door and jumped on our bikes. Behind our house was a thin trail that made its way through the tall grass and led up to the train tracks. I pumped my bike along it, while David followed.

If we wanted to, we could follow the railroad tracks and eventually we'd hit a lake. But, we weren't allowed to go to the lake by ourselves, and were sufficiently afraid of Dad to not try. He'd told us before that if he ever caught us up there he'd put his boot so far up our rears we'd taste shoe polish.

Instead, we dumped our bikes in the grass and crossed the tracks, aiming for the horse pasture on the other side. Logan was already there, waiting for us.

"Hey," he nodded and pushed his glasses up higher on his nose.

Logan and I had talked about coming here the night before, so I wasn't surprised to see him there.

"Hey," I nodded back, and pulled a grass stem to chew like I'd seen old cowboys on the TV do.

The three of us climbed up the fence and sat all casual-like. One of the horses, splotched brown and white, trotted over to us.

"You got any sugar cubes?" I asked Logan.

"What's a sugar cube?" Logan wrinkled his nose to keep his glasses from slipping.

"How the heck do I know?" I shifted on the fence. "Some type of horse food."

There was no answer. David swatted at a fly that had come along with the horse. "That horse sure is fat," he said, and then gave a big yawn.

"He looks big enough to hold my dad," Logan replied. The horse nibbled on Logan's pant leg. "Hey, leggo there." He pulled his leg away.

An idea started to grow in my mind.

This was my chance to be a real cowboy, like Little Joe.

I stood up with my heels hooked over the bottom railing of the fence,. With slow movements, I patted the back of the horse. His coat was bristly and warm under my hands. "Nice boy, good boy," I cooed in a sing-song. My heart pounded. I climbed up to the top of the fence and gently swung my leg over the horse's back.

He twitched a bit under me, but otherwise didn't move. I smiled and looked over at my brother.

"Scoot up! Make some room!" David shouted. He jumped on behind me with a quick grab around my waist.

Logan pushed at his glasses again with his thumb.

"I don't know about this, guys." He drew a deep breath in.

The horse took a few steps away from the fence and swished its tail.

"It's your loss!" David called back to him.

Logan took a giant leap and landed across the animal's hindquarters. The horse laid back its ears and gave a little snort. A second later it was galloping like it'd stepped into a fire ant's nest.

Logan fell off immediately and tumbled like one of those round weeds in the movies. I held on to its neck for dear life, and David held on to me. Neither one of us knew how to stop this blasted animal. The horse's back was darn slippery, and pretty soon we started jittering in opposite directions. David slid to one side and me on the other, the both of us staring boggle-eyed at one another from underneath the neck. David finally let go of its mane with a whoop. He rolled along neatly in the dust while I hung on. I craned my head to look and saw a fence ahead, fast approaching.

Time was up, unless I wanted to get scraped against the side of the fence. I let go and flew into a thistle bush.

Logan came running to where I was caught like a bug on fly paper. He gave me a hand and yanked me out.

"Woohooo! Did you see how that fat old honey bucket ran?"

I spit some grass from my teeth and started working on the thistles stuck in my pants. They hurt, but I wasn't going to show it.

David slapped his leg as he laughed at me. "You're sure lucky you don't have to be a cowboy! You'd starve!"

I glared at him to get him to shut up. So far, it wasn't working. "I'm gonna head home." I grumbled.

"Awww don't be a sore loser!" David said.

"I can't lose! You saw me on that horse!" I shouted back. I crossed the field and scooted under the fence.

Logan trotted after us. "Hey, don't go! There's lots more we can do."

Just then, we heard the shriek of the train whistle. The tracks took a tight corner there, and the train always slowed to take that bend.

Another idea started to form in my head. They didn't think I was brave enough to be a cowboy? I'd show them. "Want to see something cool?" I called over my shoulder.

"What?"

"What are you going to do?"

I could see the train now as it came along the curve. The vibrating noise reached right inside my guts and shook them. First, the engine chugged past and then the clang of its box cars. I started to jog alongside it. I couldn't even think about what I was going to do, otherwise I'd chicken out.

I let the cars pass me while I looked for an opportunity. A yellow one came along with a ladder welded in its side. My muscles burned as I gave an extra burst of speed, and caught the metal rung with my hand. The momentum lifted me right off my feet. I tucked my legs up and over the edge of the box car.

David and Logan's faces were white and small by the time I looked back. They started to run, but they'd never catch up. I waved at them, then the train took me round the bend and out of their sight.

Fireworks went off inside me, and I tipped my head and laughed. I couldn't believe I'd done it. I may not be famous like Dad when he played baseball, but this was almost as good.

After a quick check inside the car, I sat on the edge of the boxcar and let my legs dangle. The inside was empty and smelled damp. The floor was streaked with black stains like oil spills.

The trees flew by as the train began to pick up speed on the straight stretch. My eyebrows wrinkled as I watched the blurry grass zip past. It suddenly seemed a heap of a lot easier to jump on then off. With the way the train was accelerating, I realized the chance of getting off was about to be gone. I stood up and hung to the cars side, lurching back and forth with the momentum.

I was about to be stuck.

After a few deep breaths to steady myself, I leaped. "Geronimo!" I tucked into a ball and landed with a roll on the hill. For a few seconds, I lay there in the grass taking inventory if anything felt broken, then jumped up with a shout.

I did it! I guess I sure could ride a train even if I couldn't ride a horse.

The sun beat a hot circle on the top of my head as I walked the tracks back to David and Logan. I couldn't help but grin to think of how proud Dad would be of me, even though I couldn't chance telling him.

"Hey! A tiny shout made me look up. David was in the distance, running for me, with Logan on his trail. When my brother got closer his face relaxed with relief.

I trotted up to meet them.

"You're okay!" David put his hands on his knees and took some deep breaths. "I thought you were going to Alaska!"

"Alaska?" I said.

"Yeah! Or China!"

"Trains don't drive over the ocean, you dork."

Logan arrived just then. "Whoa, you just rode the train."

I nodded. Beat that!

The three of us walked back on the tracks. We had a contest to see who could walk the rail the longest without falling off. Logan said he won, and then David pushed him, then I said I won, and they both pushed me. When we got to our bikes, we grabbed them and peddled down the path.

I could hear Mom and Dad fighting right when we broke through the tree line into our back yard. Logan blushed and looked down at his front tire.

I darted a glance at him, heat rising to my face, too. "See ya tomorrow, okay Logan?" and spun towards the house.

Up ahead, I noticed a brand new truck in the driveway.

"Beat you there!" I shouted to David and raced towards the truck.

It was a beauty, yellow- glass flecked paint and shiny chrome trim. I dumped my bike by its bumper and rubbed my hand down the smooth fender, then swung up on the driver's step and peered inside.

Dad must have seen me because he yelled through the open kitchen window, "Ain't she pretty?" He came out to the porch with a beer in his hand.

Seeing the beer can flash in the sunlight made me feel like I was on the train again, only this time there was no way off. I grabbed the side mirror to keep from falling.

Mom was right behind him. "You're so selfish! How can you let me drive that piece of crap car and go buy yourself a new truck?"

He gave a sheepish grin, but by the sparkle in his eye I could see he was proud. He brought the beer up to his lips.

"Always easier to ask forgiveness then permission, boys," he said with a wink at us.

She kept going. "And look at that! I thought you said you were going to quit drinking?"

"I'm fine, woman."

"Maybe you want to knock a few more holes in the wall, huh?" she said, her hands cradling her belly.

He crumpled the can and threw it over his shoulder at the trash bin. It hit the rusty container and ricocheted into the grass.

"You keep this up, and you'll be jobless again!" Mom warned.

Dad walked across the yard to the truck and waved me aside with a deep frown on his face. "Get out of here. Go in to your Ma." He climbed in and started the truck, gassed it a few times so we could hear it roar, then tore down the driveway in a cloud of dust.

Mom gave a small scream of frustration. She paced in a circle, the same two lines wrinkling between her eyebrows, then called David and me over. "Get your stuff. We're going to Grandma's."

It only took a few minutes to jam our clothes into our backpacks, before climbing into Mom's faded blue Datsun. She slid her belly behind the wheel and started the car, being careful of the plywood board that lay across the rusty hole in the floor.

Chapter 4

Six months had passed and summer had arrived. I'd just turned eight, and life had taken a lot of turns for the better in the last few months. Best of all, Dad had quit drinking again.

The wind whistled through the hole in the Datsun's floor. Mom absent-mindedly nudged the board back over it with her foot, before stepping back on the gas. Her right hand rested on the baby seat next to her where my new brother, Willie, was sound asleep. She smiled when she looked at him and gave his bundled little body a couple of pats.

I leaned my head back and watched the trees fly past the window. With one eye closed, I stared down my arm balanced on the door frame. In my mind, my hand was a scythe, and I was trimming the tops of all the signs and bushes along the road's edge. Zip! Zip! Zip!

Paper crunched loudly next to me, yanking me from my reverie. I whipped my head around to look. My brother had shimmied his rear off the seat to get a rock out of his front pocket, and in his wiggling, smushed my brown lunch bag.

"You ding-bat! Look what you did!" I pointed to the wobbled up bag. I leaned over and punched his lunch.

"Ow! You dork! I didn't mean to!" He dove down on my bag landing on his elbow. He ground it in while sticking his tongue at me.

My eyebrows flew up. I grabbed his lunch and whipped it against the seat a few times before throwing it back.

He scowled and grabbed a fist full of sandwich through the bag. He squeezed it as hard as he could, leaving the bag molded like clay when he let go.

"Boys!" Mom yelled from the front seat. We both jumped with surprise. She pulled the car to the side of the road and slammed on the brakes, all of us jerking against the seat belts. "What the heck is going on back there?"

We pointed at each other and then to our destroyed lunch bags. Mom snatched the bags from us and unfolded the ruined fronts. My bag was clearly marked in black ink, "David," and his, "Jim." She rolled her eyes. "I can't believe you two." She switched the bags around and handed them back.

The two of us held our busted lunches on our laps and stared frigidly out our separate windows.

Mom looked over her shoulder for traffic and eased out on the road. She glanced in the rearview mirror at us, her face flushed with heat. "I want brotherly love here. You two pray for each other." Silence from the back seat. "I mean right now."

I sighed and started first, the well-worn prayer rolling off my tongue in monotone, "Thank you God for my brother. I forgive him."

Then it was David's turn. "Thank you God for my brother. Please help him to be a better brother."

"What?" I said, "Mom!"

He smiled. I gave him my Darth Vader glare.

Mom sighed again. "You boys better be good today. Watch out for nails. Stay out of the way. And for God's sake, quit fighting!"

Then under her breath, "What am I going to do when your dad's gone?"

Dad was leaving on a missionary trip down to Mexico with a team to build a foster-home. When I thought of him making a home for little orphaned children it made me feel all warm inside. The whole church was proud of him, and made a big deal about how he was on the right track now. I remember the pastor shaking Dad's hand, "You're a good man, and you've got a good heart. It's just that alcohol that kept you chained down."

Mom turned the Datsun down a dirt road that was surrounded by old growth fir, and we bumped along it for a few miles. Dad's yellow truck appeared up ahead, parked on the side of the road next to a driveway that disappeared uphill. Mom pulled alongside it.

"Hop out you two." She nodded to us, before rummaging in the glove box for her sunglasses. "I need to get back home to all my packing."

I flung open the door and climbed outside the car. Looking around for David, I took a big sniff of the fresh air, drawing it as deep into my body as possible. I could almost taste the thick scent of old leaves and wet grass.

Dad stepped out of his truck and walked over to her car window. They talked for a few minutes while David and I ran up the long driveway.

Mom and Dad had bought this property on the hill and were in the process of building a home. So far, we had a garage with a concrete floor and a loft. Dad had cut down four trees on the property and lined them up to use as the corner posts of the garage.

My parents weren't too far into the project when the money began to run low. Now, the new plan was to make the garage livable for us until they could afford to build the house.

Mom drove away, and Dad followed after us up the driveway. He waved us over to him. "We're clearing some rocks out of this beast."

I knew that by "beast" he meant the driveway, nearly a quarter mile long with thick ruts from the past heavy rains.

"You boys are lucky! You arrived just in time to see the show."

As soon as we got to the top I saw the offending boulder. It had a bunch of wires that escaped from of a hole drilled into its center connecting to dynamite. The wires trundled along about a hundred feet over what had once been an old river bed and disappeared inside a truck parked to one side with its hood up. A man was tinkering with the battery trying to attach the wires.

Dad whistled.

The man looked up.

"Joe! Wave to my boys."

Joe held up a hand.

"That's Joe. He's one of the new neighbors. He set up some explosives in the rock over there." I took a step towards the rock to see. "Well, hold up there, whipper-snapper. I want you boys back here." Dad waved his arm to indicate the woods. "And wait until I say it's all clear. Got it?"

David and I both nodded and ran off for the woods.

"We're just about ready now," Joe shouted to Dad.

Joe strode over to the boulder to check on the connection.

David's eyes shined at me from behind the next tree over, and I returned his grin.

"Fire in the hole!"

Joe started to run, all elbows and knees.

A brilliant light flashed through the trees. I coughed out a gasp as the enormous Whump blasted the air. It pushed me back and forced my arms up to protect my face. The explosion sucked at my eardrums, as the trees vibrated with an invisible wave.

After the echo was gone everyone around me whooped in joy. It was like the best firework ever. Their whoops cut off at the sound of rocks crashing through the branches as they fell from high in the sky. I flung my arms back across my head and curled into a ball while rocks the size of footballs smashed around me.

No one moved.

As the silence settled in I peered out through crossed arms. David peeked back at me. We both burst out in laughter.

"Look at that rock," I said. It had landed not two feet away from me, split jagged and sparkling in the sun.

Just then I felt a tickle of a creepy crawly up my leg. I shook my leg hard to jiggle it out.

"You hid on top of an anthill!" David pointed and laughed.

I waved him away and walked out to the driveway, It looked like the moon's surface, all pocked from the falling rocks.

"Did you see that, boys? That thing blew near to kingdom-come!" Dad walked around the remnants of the boulder with a happy grin. "Start clearing the rocks and stack them over to the side there." He gestured with his hands. "We've got a lot of work to do before we can move in."

I looked around and groaned. The garage needed a roof, the driveway was a mess. Heck, we still needed to get power and water up to the garage. We did have a long way to go.

*****

After gathering rocks for a while, I left David and headed up the hill to where Dad was working on the garage roof. Dad was high at the peak, straddling one of the roof supports. I climbed the ladder to the loft located under where he was at. The bottoms of my shoes made the metal ladder steps ring.

Dad and Joe crawled along the roof rafters like monkeys, as they nailed the trusses across the beams to support the roof. "One two, heave!" Their deep voices rang as they slid another truss up onto the roof and held it balanced along the roof ridge.

Dad steadied the truss against the center pole beam and reached into the leather carpenter's bag around his waist for a nail.

He lost his grip, and it began to slide. "Look out below!" he called. The truss fell on end and hit me square on the top of my head, pounding me into the loft floor like I was a nail.

Flashes of light overshadowed the pain. I reeled without control in a shroud of stars and blackness.

A tiny voice, the only part of me still able of rational thought, started to yell, "Fall down! Fall down." I was barely conscious of the edge of the loft, but realized if I went over, it would be a long way down to the concrete below. I forced my knees to buckle.

Dad jumped off the narrow rafter and down to the loft floor. "Hey? You okay?"

My ears rang in my skull. I tried to focus on his face. Dad's head swam in circles and divided into two. Vomit rose up my throat and burned. I closed my eyes.

"You're okay," Dad patted my arm. "Rub some dirt on it!" He climbed back up onto the roof. I lay there for a while until I felt like I could sit without throwing up. Slowly, I rotated to my side while my pulse thrummed in my head. I dragged myself up to my knees, then grabbed a support pole to get to my feet. After a few minutes of hanging onto the pole I slithered down the ladder to the concrete floor below, my feet missing a few steps.

My head felt heavy as I looked for a place to sit, finally staggering across the yard to a maple tree, feeling like I'd just got off the tea-cup ride at the fair. Once in the shade, I lay down with my arm flung over my eyes.

When I woke up it was dark, and Dad was calling for me.

Slowly, I crawled out from the tree and walked across the front yard to him.

"Where'd ya go?" he asked.

I pointed.

"Oh," he smirked, "lying down on the job? Don't you know a real man doesn't get hurt? You've got to be strong!"

I gently tapped the lump on my head, and he laughed and shook his head.

"Good grief, you look like a rhinoceros!" He patted me on the shoulder before pulling a soda out of his lunch pail. "Aww, you'll be okay. Here, have a drink. You look a bit parched."

I took the soda and cracked open the tab. He studied me for a second. A flash of doubt crossed his face. "You know, better not tell your Ma. She's kind of busy with the baby, and stressed about me leaving for Mexico."

I nodded.

*****

That night, I held my new baby brother, a squalling red-faced little bit that so far I'd only seen being bundled, burped, fed, or changed. He felt like a pile of beanbags in my arms. "Hey, I'm your big brother." I whispered down to him. "One day you're going to get to clean my room." His finger curled around mine, and I swear he smiled. Made my headache nearly go away.

Chapter 5

Icy snow hit the front window with sharp little ticks. Rosy, our black dog, stood up from where she'd been lying by the woodstove. She gave herself some good, hard shakes, then spun a couple of turns before she flopped back down again.

The woodstove was a beast and glowed red on the sides. But it heated the garage-house nice and toasty, even managing to warm the loft up the ladder where my brother and I had our beds.

It was a lazy day. Mom had two animal sock puppets on her hands playing with my almost two-year-old brother. I sat cross-legged at the kitchen table studying a board game, blue and red pieces set up to defend our sides. David was next to me, holding a mug of hot chocolate. Dad sat across from me and watched me with a smirk, his forefinger and thumb wiping down his mustache. We were playing Stratego.

My brain hurt from trying to defeat him. He was so good at strategizing at this game. Earlier, I'd captured his spy and finally thought I was getting the edge on him, but I still couldn't find his flag.

He jumped on my best piece still not captured. "What is it?" He had a twinkle in his eye. He knew what my piece was.

"A three," I muttered, and gave him the piece. I moved up next to his bomb. His bomb jumped me. It was a two. I scratched my head. What the heck?

In three more turns he captured all but two of my players.

"Argh!" I yelled, frustrated. I was having a hard time focusing on a new line of attack.

He looked at me and laughed. "Want to quit?"

"No!" I crossed my arms over my chest.

Dad did another move. I had one piece left on the board, and my flag.

"Fine. Whatever. I quit." I said, and leaned back from the table. "Is that your flag?" I pointed. He twirled the piece around. It wasn't the flag, but a bomb. He'd been moving his flag around like a regular piece. "Dad! You make me so mad!"

He laughed. I could tell he had played the whole game just for this moment when I figured out he was cheating. I had to laugh because he got me good.

"Alright, maybe next time you'll win." He stood up and stretched his arms overhead. "C'mon, boys! Get in the truck."

David and I stared at each other for a second, then our chairs screeched on the concrete as we scrambled from the table. We tore through our garage-house looking for jackets and boots.

My baby brother called out from the blanket on the floor. "I come too."

"Next time, mugwump," Dad said. "Hurry up, boys!"

We ran out of the house and into the frosty air. Snow was sifting off the trees in a light icy dust. My cheek stung as it blew against my face. David and I jumped into the yellow truck and tussled on the bench for a little extra room before I snapped the seatbelt around the both of us.

I was nine. I thought I should have the extra room.

The Dodge rumbled down the long driveway in deep ruts packed into the snow. Dad let go of the wheel and leaned back with his fingers laced behind his head like he was relaxing at the beach. He had a big grin on his face, this was his favorite part of the day. The steering wheel bobbled as the tires followed the quarter mile frozen channels like a train on rails.

A mushy brown slush puddle lay at the bottom.

Dad returned his hands to the wheel, pumped the gas and took the corner sharp. A spray of brown goop flew across the street splattering the mailboxes buried in the white snow bank. In the back of the truck bed, his red tool box thumped and clanged.

"I've got some work downtown. I want you boys to behave while you're there. No filly-fally." Dad talked around the cigarette gripped in the corner of his mouth.

I nodded up at Dad. David blew on his hands then jammed them into his coat pocket, elbowing me in the ribs in the process.

"Ow! You dork!"

"Ow yourself!"

Dad grinned and shook his head. "You little creeps better behave!"

We drove through town to the lake front where the water looked black under the cloudy sky.

Dad jumped out of the truck and walked around to the bed to get his tools. He nearly lost his balance when his boot found a patch of ice, and he threw his arm up to catch himself.

David and I scrambled out the other side of the truck. Dad gave a piercing whistle to catch my attention.

"Hey! You boys stay off that pier, got it? You get on it, I'll have your ass!"

We both nodded and raced towards an enormous pile of snow left by the plow. I kicked steps into the snow and climbed up. David tried to follow me.

"This is my hill!"

"Shut up! I just want to see!"

Grudgingly I scooted to one side. David climbed up and looked out at the water. A roaring growl alerted us that Dad had started his chain saw. He was getting the wood ready to build a new dock. I looked at his denim Carhartt jacket bent over the pylons.

"Dad didn't say we couldn't check out the beginning of the pier." David said. I shrugged.

We shuffled off the bank and stomped through slushy snow making giant wet sprays on our way to the lake. The water lapped gently under the pier, which floated right on top of the water.

I stood on the first board and bounced, seemed pretty safe to me.

"Hey! What's that?" David pointed to a dark mass under the water. I leaned over to look. The blob waved just under the surface, hiding beneath drifting chunks of ice. David and I got down on our hands and knees to examine it closer. It skirted beneath the pylons just out of sight. I watched for it to reappear. The mass curled out a tendril. With a ripple, it slowly made its way down the dock. Like crabs, we crept along the pier following it.

"What the heck is it?" I whispered.

"A dead body?"

"Shut up! Didn't you see the green?"

I stared hard into the water until my eyeballs hurt, the dark shadow teasing me by swaying in and out from under the pier.

David let out a frustrated sigh. He stood up, his hand on the icy railing. The edge of the landing was black with mildew, with slime leaching over the side.

"Be careful, David."

His eyes flew open. "Look!" He pointed.

I snapped my head forward to scan for the shadow. In that instant, I heard a huge splash. David had fallen in, and his panicked face bobbed among the floating ice above the shadow.

"Ahhh!" he screamed. "It's got me!" His head jerked back and disappeared underwater. I looked to Dad, but he was still working the chain saw. There was no time. I flung myself on my belly and plunged my arms into the water. I thrashed all over, smacking the cursed ice away that obscured the water's surface. Where was he? Skin touched my hand. I grasped it and yanked up with all my might.

With a suction sound, David's head broke the surface. He coughed as ice batted against his face. I grabbed the soggy shoulders of his jacket, and slowly heaved him back up onto the pier. Every tendon in my arm and back flexed at the strain, feeling close to snapping. He flopped on the wood next to me.

We sat side-by-side for a few moments, both of us deep breathing. David turned to the left and vomited water.

"You okay buddy? You all right?"

He shook his head. His brown eyes rimmed with droplets looked huge on his pale face.

"It had me," he whispered.

"What did you see down there? What was it?"

He wrapped his arms around himself.

"What had you, David?"

Slowly, he stood up, like an aching old man. His teeth chattered.

"I don't want to talk about it," he said. With dragging steps he stumbled down the pier and went to the truck. I examined the water one more time.

The shadow was gone.

Shoving my hands in my pockets, I made my way back down the dock to the truck. David's face was stone-white behind the windshield, and I could practically hear his teeth clacking away from where I was. Sighing, I glanced at Dad, who had the chainsaw deep into a log, sending a spray of sawdust against his leg and the ground.

There was no way around it. I had to tell him.

Dad looked towards the truck after I explained how David had fallen in the lake. "You're supposed to watch out for your brother." He felt around for his keys. "Go start the truck and warm him up." He tossed them at me. "Couldn't listen to me for one cursed minute." Dad patted his front pocket for a cigarette. He lit it with a flick of the match and squinted at me as he exhaled the smoke. "Don't tell your mom!"

I nodded and walked back to the truck. David watched me through the window. Wrenching the truck door open, I climbed into the driver's seat. "David, take off your jacket." I said, trying to jam the key into the ignition. The key didn't fit in, so I flipped it around and wiggled it in, before twisting it with a "snick." The engine roared to life. I jerked my hands off the steering wheel and watched the instrument panel for a moment, looking for something out of normal. We weren't moving, everything was okay.

David looked at me with tired eyes and blue lips, still clad in his wet jacket. Huffing a deep breath, I leaned across the gear shift, grabbed his sleeve and tugged on the jacket. It finally peeled away, and I chucked it with a wet smack to the floor. Quickly, I shrugged out of my own wool-lined jacket and wrapped it around David's shoulders. It wasn't perfect because my sleeves were wet, but it still seemed to warm him up. I spun the heater dial to high and rubbed his arms. The heat blasted against us, lifting our hair.

"There, you'll be alright."

David shivered less as he warmed up. Soon we were back to pushing each other for hogging up the seat.

I never did learn what he saw under that pier.

*****

When we got home David was all back to being pink and warm. Dad never said a word, and neither did my brother and I. Mom asked Dad if we'd been good. He looked over at us and his lip curled a bit under his moustache. "Oh you know. Boys'll be boys."

"Well, they must have been busy, they both look worn out!" Mom said as she set plates of chili and cornbread in front of us.

Man, was I ever, and David too, judging from the dark circles under his eyes. It wasn't long after a dinner that we both crawled up the ladder into the loft and went to our beds.

Still, all it took was a good night's sleep and we were raring to go the next day. The pier was forgotten.

Dad was whistling when we came down the ladder the next morning. Mom stirred a pot on the stove.

"Eat your oatmeal boys." Dad said. "I've got a surprise for you when you're done."

I drizzled maple syrup on my oatmeal, then took a big bite. David skipped the syrup. He gulped his down with giant spoonfuls just to try to beat me. It made me kind of cross to see him try, so I picked my bowl up and finished it in two massive swallows. I smiled when I set the bowl down, but it was soon wiped away when I saw his spoon spinning around an empty bowl too, and him smiling back at me.

Dad pulled our jackets off from the hooks where they'd been hanging by the wood stove to dry all night. David's had a weird green film on the white stripes. He threw them at us like a horseshoe toss and told us to hurry up; we were going down to Elias and Ruby's house.

"Elias has a great sledding spot, boys! Let's go!" David and I scrambled into our snow gear and headed out the door.

Mom wouldn't let Willie go. "You're still too little." He cried, but she soothed him with a cookie.

When we got outside Dad showed us his surprise. He'd built us a sled out of a pair of skis screwed into the legs of an old coffee table. I eyeballed it, feeling skeptical. That thing looked a tad sketchy.

Dad hooted when he saw my face, "What! Haven't you ever seen a bobsled before? I guess not one like this! This one here has a name, Dynamo!"

I snorted at the name. Dad arched an eyebrow in my direction and said, "You just wait and see. I'll betcha you'll be yelling 'Dynamo' going down the hill on this sucker!"

"I'll bet I'll be yelling something!" I flipped back. He chuckled.

Half the neighborhood was already there when we arrived. Elias had the steepest driveway around. He and his brother had been up late at night pouring water to turn it into the slickest hill ever, and the ice glistened in the sun. Dad dragged the coffee table with a rope, struggling with his footing to get to the top, with us two following behind. Once there, he pushed the sled into position and gave it a few shakes to instill some confidence in us with its sturdiness. "Hop on boys!"

I looked at David and we both shrugged. There was nothing to do but to get on. We had a little scuffle over who'd ride in the front before we settled down. Dad handed me the rope. "Ready?" he asked.

I'd hardly nodded before he gave the sled a huge push. To say that we flew down the hill on that old coffee table balanced on skis, would be an understatement. All I saw was a white blur, with a dark blur at the bottom that I knew must be avoided at all costs.

As we hurtled towards the trees the bobsled started to rattle and jerk. I pulled on the rope hoping it would slow us down, and it came off in my hands.

"Mmm Mmmm Mmmake iiiiiiit Sto stop!" David vibrated in my ear. I was a bit confounded just how to do that. Two of the coffee table legs began to bend forward, while the other two bent backwards. I clenched my jaw to keep my teeth from snapping together.

The bottom of the driveway took a bit of a turn, so the decision of where to stop was real easy. One set of legs continued on without us as the rest of the coffee table imbedded like a torpedo into the bank. I cartwheeled through the air, landing first on my shoulder, then my head, and finally on my back. Once I quit moving, I thought it might be a good idea just to rest there a while. Somewhere nearby David crowed, "Look at me! I'm making a snow angel!"

From up the top of the hill Dad's voice echoed down, filled with glee. "Dyyynamo!"

Chapter 6

I never was really good at reading out loud. Unfortunately, for Mr. Bentley, my fifth grade teacher, being able to read out loud was his proof that you actually learned the work. So we did it, a lot. He always seemed to pick on the most nervous kid. Right at this moment, that was me.

"Any day now would be nice." Mr. Bently stared at me with dark eyes that seemed to want to rip my soul right out of my throat.

He'd asked me to read the first five paragraphs of the Constitution and I was frantically flipping through my history book.

"Where were you when I told the rest of the class to turn to the Constitution? How come you're the only one who can't follow along?"

I could feel my throat start to swell. The pages in the textbook stuck together and the numbers blurred as I tried to find where it was.

Not here, no, not here either.

Around me desks squeaked as kids turned in their chairs to look.

"Well, Jim? I don't think you're even trying." Mr. Bently said through clenched teeth. He picked up the chalkboard eraser and rolled it back and forth in his hands.

Sweat trickled down the back of my neck.

"Ww We the people..."

Smack! Mr. Bently flung the eraser at me. I grabbed my forehead after it bounced off my scalp. My chest tightened until I started to shake. I didn't dare look up.

The silence in the classroom was electrified with fear.

"What are you? Stupid? I said Article I. Turn to page twenty-eight." He walked over and stood in front of me.

I turned to the page. "All Legislative Powers..."

"Jim!" He slammed his hands on the desk, and I jumped. "I won't have any of your mumbling. Begin again."

I wanted to puke as I started over.

I don't remember how I got through the rest of that class.

After the bell rang I ran down the hallway. Standing in front of the trophy case, I gave a quick look around. When the coast was clear, I slipped out the front door to the school parking lot and sprinted left down the sidewalk to ShopRite, afraid to look back in case I'd be caught.

Mom worked in the ShopRite grocery store deli. Her eyes widened as I tore down the aisle headed for the back where the deli was.

"What on earth?" She started to say as I whipped around the counter and grabbed her waist in a big bear hug. She smelled like laundry soap and fried chicken. I breathed in deeply.

Her hand automatically patted my back, "What's going on, Jim?"

I didn't want to talk for a minute. I just wanted to hide away. She rotated the both of us to shield me from anyone watching and whispered in my ear, "Tell me what's the matter."

I told her what'd happened.

"Again?" Her arms stiffened around me, and she gave my back a firmer pat then she meant in her anger. "How dare he! That's it!" She spun away from me with her hands in the air and puffed her cheeks. After taking a few steps in a tight circle, she said, "You go sit over there for a minute, Jim," and pointed to the break room. "I'm calling the principal."

She stomped the length of the counter to the phone, my heart smiling with each step. Yeah! Go get him!!

The two lines between her eyebrows formed a deep frown as she seized the receiver off the wall and dialed. She tapped her foot as it rang, then, "Mr. Newton. Do you know what one of your teachers just did?" Her hand clenched the front of her apron. "He threw an eraser at my son and called him stupid. I'm done, that teacher's been a bully one too many times. Jim's not going back to class." She paused, listening. "No, I don't care to transfer him to another room." She whirled around and her voice got deep with anger. "I'll find him another school that's half-way decently run. This is bull crap." Slamming the phone down, she looked at me.

I stared back, unsure of what just happened.

"All right, we'll figure this out." She took a few easy breaths, and patted her hair. "You just sit tight for now. Want a piece of chicken?"

I waited in the break room until her shift ended, feeling a bit like a celebrity as the other workers came in and talked with me. Words flew over my head as they drank their cups of coffee; "Threw an eraser at him." "What is this world coming too?" "Called him stupid!" "You know, last week my daughter's teacher up and walked out of the classroom. They still don't have a new one!"

Mom ended up pulling David from school too. She brought home a catalogue of curriculum that her missionary friend had used when they were in Africa. Every night, she poured through it with a spiral notebook, making a list of the books she wanted. I was a mite scared at how long that list was getting, and wondered if she'd notice if I erased a few. She seemed to read my mind because the next time I looked, the notebook was gone.

A box arrived about a week later carried to the door by a red-faced UPS man who looked fit to be tied at the thought of having to back his truck down our rutted driveway.

Mom thanked him and then, groaning, she pushed the big box across our concrete floor. "Boys! Hurry! Come see what just came!" She clapped her hands like it was a Christmas present to open, and told David to bring her a knife. My stomach felt kind of heavy. That box was a lot bigger than I'd expected.

David brought a knife.

Mom took it from him, then carefully slid it under the tape. I glanced at David with a deadpan face. Mom pushed back the box flaps and cooed, "Would you look at that!" She gave a happy humming sound while lifting out the books. When she was done, they were organized into two neat piles. I frowned. My pile was considerably taller than David's. Mom patted the covers with satisfaction.

Dad came in from outside to wash his hands. He glanced at the pile on his way through to the kitchen.

"What's all this?"

"The boy's school books."

"Hmmmp," Dad turned off the water and searched for a dish towel. "You boys gonna do your school at home?"

He had a half smile that his moustache couldn't quite hide.

"Yep." I answered, suddenly not too keen.

Dad snorted. "Don't get your hopes up, Ma. You know how boys are."

Mom shooed him out of the house and then cleared the clean laundry pile off of the kitchen table to the sofa. Still humming, she set my books on the left, paused to look, then straightened the pile a bit more.

She couldn't stop looking at David's covers with their colorful cartoon animals holding balloons. She flipped to lesson one, a simple printing exercise.

"So fun!" she said to herself. Smiling, she pointed to the empty chairs and said in a Sunday-School teacher voice, "Sit! We've got a lot of work to catch up on."

The happy voice was strained by noon, then lunch helped bolster her spirits. But, by the time we got to Math ("What in the world is 'New Math,'" she grumbled.) the Sunday-School voice disappeared, never to return.

That was our first day.

Over all, the first week went pretty well, with us hitting all of our core school subjects. But, that wouldn't be repeated, and every week after that was a crazy mess. Mom would sit us down in the morning to explain the assignments for the day. She could hardly get five words out before my youngest brother, Willie, asked her for something. Just as soon as she was done helping him she'd look at her watch and realize she was late for work, and run to change, her pink bathrobe flapping.

The next time we'd see her she had Willie's hand firmly in hers, towing him out the door to drop him off at Grandma's. She'd turn around and shout, "Get your work done. You boys be good!" and she was off.

This particular morning I was learning about how to diagram a sentence. It'd only been about a half hour since Mom had left, and already the words were swimming on the page. I rubbed my eyes to focus. What the heck was an adverb? Who even cares? A yawn about broke my face in half. I fidgeted in my chair, then stretched to wake up.

David was pouring over his math book with rumpled eyebrows, while his fingers tapped his whispered numbers on the paper. He was so preoccupied that he didn't notice me watching him.

With a grin, I slapped the table as hard as I could. He jumped and stared wide-eyed, then socked me in the arm.

"Don't you punch me!" I grabbed his hands and pushed them away.

"You scared me!"

I laughed. "Books aren't going to teach us how to get what we want from life." After Mr. Bently, I didn't want to see another book again. "C'mon, let's get out of here."

He slammed his book shut and flipped the pencil across the room. "Woohooo!"

We laced up our tennis shoes and then ran for the door, both of us getting hung up for a moment when we tried to get through it at the same time.

It was a glorious day, one of those days meant for living outside. The sun was so bright it made me squint, and I yanked down my baseball cap. It smelled like summer even though it was early May. Our dog, Rosy, lay in the shade of the house and thumped her tail in the dirt when she saw us. I gave her a whistle while I grabbed my bike from the side of the greenhouse, but she wasn't going anywhere. My bike seat was hot when I jumped on, so I stood on the pedals and sped off down the driveway. David was right behind.

We raced up and down the street pumping the pedals as fast as we could. About a mile down the road I skidded to a stop.

There was a piece of plywood lying in the ditch.

David and I dragged it out and propped it up on some rocks to build a little ramp. We spent the rest of the morning zipping off the jump and pretending we were Evel Knievel leaping over cars.

The sun was directly overhead when David announced he was roasting hot and needed a break. He dumped his bike in the middle of the road and flopped down on the grass. I rode around his blue bike once, and it irked me to see it there.

"Better move your bike, David."

He shrugged and rolled onto his back holding a grass blade to his lips.

"I swear I'll run it over."

He blew a sharp whistle through the blade.

I pedaled up the hill. At the top I saw he hadn't listened to me, and the bike was still lying there.

"That little creep doesn't believe me," I muttered.

I took my foot off the pedal and started to coast the hill. About halfway down I was pedaling as fast as I could, the baseball cards in my spokes rumbling like a motorcycle. I wanted to give him a scare he wouldn't forget. His bike was lined up with my front tire and I called out, "Here I come!"

He sat up on his elbows to watch me. I'd planned to swerve at the last second, but, suddenly I was going too fast to change directions without wiping out. When I hit that bike I flew right over his seat in a way that would've made Ol' Evel proud, and sent the seat skittering across the road like a top.

David's mouth dropped open like a fly trap.

"Hey! That was my new bike seat!"

"Told you I'd hit it if you didn't move it!" I felt bad, but I couldn't say it. David snatched the seat off the ground with a glare and stuffed it under his arm. He jumped on his bike and stood on the pedals all the way home.

Dad was there when we rode up to the house. I was sort of surprised to see him off work so early, and felt a familiar pinch in my chest. He was half under his truck giving something underneath there a whack. Curse words punctuated each blow.

David chucked his bike seat against the shed with a thump and stomped over to tell Dad what I'd done.

Dad pulled himself out from beneath the truck with a scowl. He had grease and sweat on his face. It didn't look like a good time to mess with him.

Dad didn't blink during the entire tale. "Well, you know where the wrenches are. Fix it."

David looked daggers at me and kicked a rock on his way to the shed.

Dad burped, then signaled at me. "Jim! Look behind the seat, and get me my black tire iron."

I wrenched the yellow truck door open and leaned over the back of the seat. I froze, like a rattle snake was curled up there ready to strike. Propped next to the tire iron was a 5th of whiskey. It looked nearly empty. I swallowed. There was another empty bottle tilted next to it. I felt queasy as I grabbed the iron.

When I held it out to dad, I couldn't meet him in the eye.

He yanked it from my hand and slid back under the truck. There was a clink, and his feet scrambled for purchase in the dirt as he applied pressure.

SNAP!

The iron gave a loud clunk as it slipped off the nut, and the truck shuddered. "Son of a bitch!" he yelled.

I took a few steps back.

The engine crashed and vibrated as he beat on the undercarriage. He pulled himself out like a red-faced troll and flung the tire iron across the yard. It flew end-over-end through the air and vanished into the black berry bushes.

David peeked his head out from behind the shed door for a moment, his brown eyes taking in the scene, before he disappeared back inside.

Dad looked around wildly for something to strike at. He knocked over his tool box with a kick that sent the tools flying into the dirt, then stumbled into the house.

It was a relief to see him go. I bent down to pick up a socket and wiped the dust off on my pants.

Just then there was a familiar grinding rattle sound in the air. Mom's car bumped up the driveway home from work. Crap! I ran behind a cracked green planter.

The car stopped with a cloud of dust that floated by my hiding place. She got out and pulled out her purse, before popping the back seat. A loud crash along with a string of curse words came from inside the house. She froze and looked across the driveway at Dad's truck. Her shoulders wilted. Willie came squirming out from the back seat chattering away about Grandma's house. She took his hand and they disappeared inside.

Rosy walked over to where I was and gave me sweet eyes, so I squatted down and hugged her. I didn't want to go in. I didn't want to hear them fight and fail again by not picking sides.

Another crash came from the house, and then their angry voices carried over to where I was. Mom yelled, "Why don't you just go to the bar then?"

Dad shouted back, "Shut the hell up!" The door slammed, and he came out with Mom's car keys. He jumped into her car and ground the gears, and flew down the driveway with the car spitting gravel from the tires. I wouldn't see him again that night.

A tap on the shoulder made me jump. David was suddenly next to me from where he'd been hunkering down in the shed. I'd forgotten about him. His eyes took half his face, and he sighed. I gave him a pat on the shoulder, wishing I'd taken him away earlier so he wouldn't have heard them.

"It'll be okay. Let's go fix your bike. We'll pretend we're Daytona mechanics."

The front door opened again. This time it was Mom who called us to come in the house. "You boys get in here now and show me your papers!"

We both groaned. There was still music to face about the unfinished schoolwork.

Chapter 7

Clattering pans on the stove woke me up. I rolled over and looked at David, wrapped like a blanket burrito in his bed with just a tuft of hair sticking out the top. Downstairs, Mom was cooking breakfast. "Get up, Boys! It's not Spring Break yet!"

Groaning, I sat up. We'd been homeschooling for three months, and it already felt like forever. Dad whistled the tune to some TV show as he got his things together to leave for work. Then, he was out the door. I grabbed a t-shirt out from under my pillow and yanked it over my head, before crawling to the ladder. With my feet on the outside of the rungs, I slid down.

Willie had just turned four, and sat swinging his legs at the table with a stack of pancakes steaming in front of him. I pulled up a chair next to him. The house smelled cozy and reminded me of Christmas time.

Mom flipped a cake onto a plate and set it before me. "My word, Jim! Check out your morning hair!" she said with a smile.

I tried to smooth it down real quick and reminded myself to go look for a baseball cap later.

David came clunking down the ladder with a grumpy face. He slumped into his chair and rested his cheek on a hand, pushing his eye all squinty. I ignored him and grabbed the peanut butter to grease my cakes. A second later I reached for the syrup too, but Willie snatched it from me.

"Gimme that, you have enough," I said, wrenching the syrup bottle away.

"Mom!"

"Boys, you better share." She glanced at her watch.

"Oh my word! I'm late, again! David, get your science done today. I mean it this time! I'm not joking." She pointed a finger at me. "Jim, work on your math, and for heaven's sake, print neater. It looks like you dipped a chicken in ink and let her walk all over your paper. Willie, be good for your brothers." She took her last swig of coffee and set the cup in the sink. After kissing each of us on the tops of our head, she grabbed her purse off from the chair and hurried out.

David pushed away from the table and walked over to the stove with sluggish steps. There was one remaining pancake in the pan.

"Guess this one's mine huh?" he said glumly.

"Hurry up and eat!" I said. "I've got big plans for us today."

I took my plate to the sink, and then walked to the little cubby that housed the washing machine.

Mom had finished a load that morning, and it sat overflowing in the wicker laundry basket. I tipped it towards me; it was a load of whites. Yes! I wiped my sticky hands on the back of my pants and grabbed the wicker basket. Carrying it across the living room to the couch I called to my brothers. "Sock war!"

They scrambled away from the table. David inspected the laundry and began to sort out all the socks. I went to the wall outlet to plug in the overhead fan. Dad had meant to wire it in to a switch a long time ago, but instead had left the wire bare and hanging. I grabbed the two wires and jammed the stripped copper into the outlet. SNAP! A few sparks. And the fan was in motion. Only one speed; High.

David had pulled out a good amount of socks by now and scrunched them up into balls. They looked like a pile of snowballs. We lay on our backs and took aim at the spinning fan blades.

"Fire!" I commanded.

Three balled up sock missiles shot up. The fan swatted them across the room like a batter behind home plate. Willie and David had a brief argument about whose sock went the furthest, before we aimed again.

We did a few rounds of this until we grew bored. Socks were strewn all over the house, and the basket of laundry was scattered across the couch. David flopped down on the pile of clothes.

"All right, guys," I said. "Outside. It's time for my master plan." That perked up their ears. My brothers stuffed their feet into their muddy shoes left by the door and followed me outdoors.

I grabbed the shovel from where it'd been leaning against the porch. Dad had used it last week to dig out the garden, which is what had given me the idea.

I marched to the middle of the yard.

"Under my feet is the world's greatest military fort." My brothers blinked at me. "C'mon, let's dig it out, and have all the neighbor kids come over. We'll have the best Army game ever!"

They jumped up with loud whoops, excited to make our yard the envy of the neighborhood gang.

David ran to the greenhouse and grabbed the other shovel. Willie was left with Mom's gardening trowel and he frowned as he held it. I told him he could be point man during our army game which reduced the sting.

We started to dig. The dirt was easy to move because it was mostly sand.

"This is going to be the best foxhole ever!" David declared. Sand was plastered across half his face and sprinkled throughout his hair.

We burrowed deeper and deeper. Soon we were hauling out five gallon buckets of excavated dirt with a rope. We didn't want to stop because it was so hot outside, and it was cool at the bottom of the hole.

When we couldn't see over the top of the pit we decided it was deep enough. David and I tugged a piece of plywood left over from the roof out of the blackberries. We dropped it on top of the hole with a loud, "Fwop!" and covered it with dirt and branches.

It was awesome.

Dad drove up the driveway, home from work. He climbed out of the truck, pausing when he saw the branch mound in the front yard.

"What the heck is that?" He walked over, his face emotionless.

My two brothers both spun around to look at me. I could read their eyes; "This is all on you, Bub."

"Umm, a foxhole." I answered.

"How deep?" He nudged the plywood up to inspect the inside.

"Maybe, mmm, three feet," I hedged a little, unsure of how he'd take this info.

"I'm thinking five." he said dryly. He stared at each of us. We shifted back and forth under his gaze. Then a tiny smile appeared at the corner of his mouth. "Now, you can enjoy burying it all back up again." He winked at me, with that smile that meant he was proud. I loved it when Dad was sober.

*****

It didn't last long. Dad came home just before dinner time the next night drunk and angry. None of us knew why he was so mad.

There was a furious look in Dad's eyes as he walked into the kitchen with a whiskey bottle in his hand. Chills ran up my spine, and I backpedaled away from him to join Mom and my brothers in the living room corner of the garage-house.

"Dammit to hell!" he shouted. His eyes appeared black when he looked around. Catching his reflection in the kitchen window he punched the glass with a "Twack!" The double panes quivered but the glass held. Obscenities poured out of his mouth, dark and vicious as he swung his head searching for something to throw.

I wanted to puke.

This was not my dad, this was a madman. And when he appeared, we all knew to hide. Mom had all us boys sheltered behind her in the living room as she watched him guardedly. None of us made a sound. We were afraid to even move and attract his attention. My muscles started to shake, from fear or adrenaline, I didn't know.

He twisted from the window and stumbled over to the table. His arm lashed out and swept the dishes clattering to the floor. He lifted the whiskey bottle for a swig, dribbling it down his front, and then wiped his mouth on the back of his arm. With a growl he slammed the bottle on the counter. I couldn't believe it didn't shatter, and he glared at it like he was mad it hadn't. His eyebrows furrowed as his fist clenched.

"Tell me I have demons," he slurred. "Where's Pearl? You tell me I have demons?" He took another gulp off the bottle before peering into it. "They taste pretty damn good to me." In a funny side-step forward he tripped on his own dragging feet. He flung his hand down where he thought the table ought to be and fell over on a rolling cup.

"Confound son of a bitch! Son of a… Where are my sons? C'mere boys and help your old man up."

Mom tightened her arms around us, but she needn't worry. We didn't move a muscle.

Dad pulled himself up with one worn hand on the table. "Forget it, I'll do it myself. I don't need anybody."

Mom let go of us. "Run for the car." We all ran, with me being the last one out. Every other time we left I'd always given a quick glance at Dad, hoping he'd care that we were leaving.

This time I didn't look back.

*****

We'd been doing this more and more often. I didn't mind going to Grandma's house. She lived out in the woods in a little trailer. Behind the trailer was a dark shed. That's where the magic happened. We'd crack open the door of the shed to see bottle after bottle of Grandpa's homemade Dynamite root beer. If Grandpa was in a good mood he'd give us a bottle. That stuff was dynamite too. There were quite a few explosions that went off on warm days when the carbonation tore the bottle apart.

On this occasion, we stayed there for a week.

On the way back home to our house on the hill I wondered what Dad would say. He usually acted like nothing happened when we returned after a few days away.

Mom pulled into the yard. Dad's truck was already sitting there. Just as soon as she turned the car off, David and I yanked the doors open, and the three of us scattered. None of us wanted to be in the vicinity to hear the fighting begin.

I sprinted, with my brothers behind, for the far back yard where we kept the pigs. Mom had got them for my brother this year for 4-H. Dad had rigged an electric fence around the pen, and it sure would jolt you if you accidentally touched it. David tried to talk Willie into urinating on it, but even at four, Willie was too savvy for that trick.

The pigs ambled up to us making soft grunting noises. David reached through the fence with a long stick and gave the pig's bristly back a scratch. There was food in the trough, so that meant Dad had taken care of them while we were away. That kind of made me feel steadier inside, to think Dad was back to normal.

We headed into the shade of the deep woods. David ran over to the grove of vine maples and started shimmying up one, getting halfway to the top before his weight pulled the skinny tree down. From there he could reach the ground and jump, and have the tree spring him back up before bouncing him down again. Willie wanted to try so I had to find him a tiny maple. I didn't want the tree to fling his body into kingdom-come. Then we'd really catch it from Mom.

We bounced for a while then straddled the bent trees like horses.

"Want to check out the haunted house?" I asked.

"Yeah, why not," David answered. Willie knew he was the youngest and didn't even try to have a say.

The people we'd bought the property from had built a two story house deep in the forest. For some reason, they'd decided to abandon the house and moved into a trailer on the other side of the woods.

There was no real path to the house, but we knew where it was. Through the years, we'd explored every inch of the forest. I led the way around the vine maples, heading in the same direction that moss grows on trees. We saw some fresh deer droppings and looked around for a minute with interest, but when no deer materialized we continued forward.

The house sat back in the gloom of old growth trees. There were blackberries that clung to the outside of it, even creeping into the house through broken windows, like determined intruders.

I opened the door, and we all walked into the musty living room feeling as though we'd stepped back in time. The wallpaper was faded near white in places, with pictures hanging crooked and forgotten. We kept our eyes open for any pit-falls, because the floor had sunk in spots through the years. Walking across the floor reminded me of being in the fun house at the fair.

David started up the stairs, so Willie and I followed after him. There were rat droppings scattered on the steps, and I heard scurrying in the wall behind the banister. I shivered, then tried to cover by pulling the front of my shirt straight.

Upstairs, the vents had all been removed from the floor and thrown in a pile next to a battered bookcase. We previously had used the vent holes like spy look-outs. Willie stuck his head through now to peer down to the floor below.

"Hey! Look at me!" He giggled, muffled by the floor.

"What is that, a spider?" I asked David. Willie pulled his head out right quick, his hair sticking up and covered in dust bunnies. He looked from side to side for the spider, trying to appear casual.

"Huh?" David asked.

I grinned. "Never mind."

"Hey I know! Let's play hide and seek," David's eyes darted to different corners, already searching for a place to hide.

I felt a thrill at the thought. Rats made it even scarier.

"I don't want to," Willie said. We didn't want him to tattle, so we agreed.

The house had settled a bit more since the last time we'd been in it, and the back wall looked different to me. I walked over to check it out, careful to step around a moldy photo album and some broken dishes.

The wall had a dark crack that ran vertically up it, just wide enough for me to fit my finger in.

"Hey Guys!" I yelled. "Come here quick!"

Both of my brothers came running. On his way, Willie got tangled up in something rope-like on the floor. He let out a howl as he tripped, but leaped back up. A pair of pantyhose was wrapped around his shoe.

David immediately saw what I was so excited about. "Wow," he drawled out.

Cautiously, I reached out and slid my fingers into the space, then pulled on the crack.

The wall was on hinges. It opened with a creak to reveal a gloomy room. I couldn't see the back, and the entrance was full of spider webs.

"Oh my gosh! It's a freaking secret room!" I was knocked almost breathless by the treasure.

"Holy Cow!" David's eyes were huge, and he started to laugh. "Right out of Scooby Doo!"

"What do you think they made it for?" I wondered out loud.

A spider lazily dropped down from the top of the wall frame where it had been disturbed.

All three of us stared at it. It waggled its eight legs at us, then turned its bulbous body to crawl back up its silk.

"I think that thing has hair." I whispered.

"I think he has a first name." David said.

Willie whispered "Charlotte." We both snapped our eyes down at him.

"Charlotte? I don't think so." I shook my head. "Maybe Bubba."

"Whatever." David gave me a little push. "You going in there, or what?"

From the back corner of the secret room came a squeak, then feet furiously moving.

"Mom always says the first shall be last," I retorted, still not taking my eyes off the spider.

"Finders keepers... after you," David countered.

I swallowed. It was a secret room after all. "It'd be cool to stick up one of those pictures with the cut out eyeholes, and hide back here to spy," I said, and warily stuck my head into the room.

There was another squeak and a rattle of rodents fighting in one of the dark corners. It gave me the heebie-jeebies, and I shuddered. That creeped-out David, which set off Willie. Shivering, we all lurched away from the secret room, violently brushing our arms and hair. I gave the wall a kick shut on my way out.

That finished the adventure for me, and I galloped down the stairs to the porch with my brothers right behind. David collapsed on a dusty wood box. Willie and I sat on the porch swing. We stayed until it was nearly dark outside, trying to stretch our time away. None of us wanted to admit we were avoiding going back home.

The moon rose and shone through the alders, making shadows on the front of the house.

"Well, I guess we should go. There's school tomorrow," I said.

"Yep, and dinner too." David nodded. We got up, and I grabbed a walking stick from the porch railing.

"Maybe Mom made fried chicken?" Willie picked up a rock and threw it at a tree.

"Remember that story of Dad?" David asked me.

I nodded. "You mean when he was six."

Willie was walking in front of us and turned around. "Wait? What is it?"

I chopped at the tall grass in front of me with my stick. "Dad was out in the rain playing in some holly field. He got cold and wet, and so he prayed, "Lord, when I get home I just want a new pair of shoes and some fried chicken.""

David cut in. "So when he got home, Grandma had chicken in the frying pan, and moccasins sitting on the table."

"I don't like moccasins." Willie frowned. "But I'll take the chicken!"

I laughed. "Don't think you need to worry about that."

*****

Mom had put the white tablecloth on the table and was just pulling a casserole out of the oven when we came inside. The tablecloth signified she wanted a "gentleman dinner," which meant we'd better use our manners, or catch it.

Dad nodded to me. "Come help me get haul in some wood."

I followed him outside to the wood pile.

"So," Dad stacked a few logs in my arms. "Did you have fun at your grandma's?"

"Yep."

"Good." He smiled at me. "What'd you do? What'd you guys talk about?"

I licked my lips and juggled the logs. He wasn't asking me questions to see if I enjoyed my time there. He knew it wasn't a vacation.

"Root beer," I answered, and brought the load of wood in.

Chapter 8

"You know Jim, you ain't as smart as you think you are."

We were relaxing in the treehouse when Darrell, the kid from up the road, said this. I tipped back my can of soda and took three big gulps.

"Yeah? Why's that?"

Darrell dragged his sleeve across his nose. "I'm just saying I know how to build hidey-holes too."

I laughed. I knew exactly the type of hidey-holes and camouflage Darrell made. It was the summer of my 11th year, and nearly every day we'd met out in the woods and pretended we were soldiers. We were supposed to hide from each other, but I always found him right away, a fern sticking out of his hair and a maple twig stuck in his pocket.

He got up to stretch his legs.

"Watch out for the trap door." I warned.

"I'm watching, I'm watching." He leaned across David to grab a soda out of the paper grocery sack. "Where's that cigarette?"

We'd filched one earlier from Dad's open pack on the buffet. We'd only done it a time or two before, and always did it as a group so none of us could tell. I patted my pocket to answer. Darrell reached over for it.

Whoosh!

He half disappeared through the hole in the floor.

"Help! Help!" he squealed. His one good leg was bent at the knee clear up to his ear, while the other leg kicked up a storm below. He tried to push up with his palms, but was wedged in too tight to budge.

I looked over at David. In the next second we were howling with laughter.

"You guys! You buttheads! Help!" His face turned red from the effort of trying to get free.

Tears ran down our faces.

"You look like a squawking chicken!" David yelled.

I wiped my eyes with the bottom of my t-shirt, then leaned over and gave him my hand. With my foot braced against the tree I hauled him back up. He was shaking as he stood next to me and gave me a shove on the shoulder.

"Next time watch where you're stepping." I grinned.

He muttered and went back to his soda can.

"Maybe I should go home," he said.

"Maybe. I think I hear your mom calling!" David giggled.

"Naw, you're ok, just relax for a minute." I took my own advice and settled back against the tree trunk.

There was rustling below the trap door. We quieted down to listen. The ladder shook, and Dad's head appeared. "What's all that tee-heeing I hear up here?" His brown eyes sparkled clear. I breathed a sigh of relief and my stomach unclenched. Sober.

Darrell still looked cross, but David and I answered, "Nothing!"

Dad found a smashed cigarette butt under some old cans and held it up between his thumb and forefinger. "Well, ain't this interesting?"

I was suddenly absorbed in picking out a splinter stuck in my palm.

Dad flicked it away. "Well, come on down. I got an idea."

David and I rushed down the ladder, knocking in to one another. Darrell came down a little more careful. He limped for a few moments until we left him behind, then jogged to catch up.

We followed Dad to the side of the property, out where an old car had been abandoned years ago. The car had been there so long it had saplings that grew through the floorboards and stretched out the passenger window. I smacked the rusty hood as I passed, causing David and Darrell to imitate me. We climbed up the hill where Dad waited for us at the top. Laid out on the ground was a thick rope, a pulley, and a little metal cable car seat.

I prodded the rope with my foot. David squatted down to pick up the pulley and gave the metal wheel a spin. He rolled it up and down his leg like a match box car.

"So here's what's up, boys." Dad arched his eyebrow and swung his arm to point. "I'm going to tie this rope to this tree here, string it all the way down the hill and attach it to that tree down there." He rubbed his hands together. "I figure we can get a good cable car going."

I had a little tingle growing inside. The bobsled popped to mind.

Dad looped the rope in a figure eight around the trunk and its branch. When he had it good and tight he started down the hill unwinding the rope as he went.

We barreled after him, crashing into bushes on our way. One had stickers that tore a good size hole in my t-shirt. I stuck my finger through the hole. Cool!

When he got to the bottom Dad went straight for the other tree. He examined it for a moment, his head tipped back. "Yup, this'll work." With a big jump, he caught a branch and pulled himself up, his work boots knocking off bits of bark. Then he leaned down, his hand wagging impatiently.

"Pass me that rope!"

I stretched on my toes to reach it to him. Once he had hold of it he pulled some slack and coiled it over his arm a few times, then started to climb higher.

"I want to be just high enough so that your butts don't hit the ground when the rope stretches."

From where we stood he sure looked plenty high. He straddled the crook of a thick branch and knotted the rope around the trunk.

"There we go." Grunting, he gave the rope an extra hard jerk in the final knot. "That'll hold nice."

He climbed down with another shower of bark and dusted himself off. We all followed him back up the hill like a line of baby ducks after the mom.

At the top, he tugged on the rope to feel how taut it was, and the corners of his mouth turned up with satisfaction. He grabbed the pulley from David and gave it a spin that made it sing, "whrrrrr."

Gently, he set the pulley on the rope, as though it were a crown being placed on the head of a king. "There we go. There it is," he whispered.

He looped the metal cable through the pulley, and yanked it down. With some quick movements, he attached it to the seat.

"Wooo wee! We did it boys!" He vibrated with excitement, and his glance ping-ponged between us. "So, who's going to be the first for a ride?"

I walked over and looked down the steep hill to the other end and then back to the seat positioned kind of precarious on the rope.

I took a step back and kept my mouth shut tight.

"What are you worried about?" Dad gave a crooked grin. "Haven't I always told you that you don't need to worry as long as you look up?"

I gave the barest of nods.

David jumped up. "I will, Dad!"

"Okay, great! Now, you just sit your fanny right on there." Dad held the seat by the harness while my brother clambered on. David's legs jogged up and down as the seat bobbled under his weight. The pulley gave a sharp creak. David's eyes shot up at it, and he swallowed.

"Naw, it's all good." Dad said. "Just the rope stretching." David's knuckles whitened from his grip on the harness. "You ready? One, two, three!" On three, Dad gave the seat a mighty shove.

We watched, impressed, as the cable car shot off. It quickly increased speed. The squealing of the pulley carried right up the hill, sounding like a pig late for dinner. I wondered if it would spark and catch the rope on fire. David stoically faced the tree, his legs braced in front of him.

"How's he going to stop?" Darrell whispered to me. I couldn't answer. Just at that moment the seat gave a little half-turn, and David spun to face us. His eyes were huge and his mouth even bigger.

We all started yelling, "Spin back David!" "Quick!"

There was no time to change directions. With a loud smack, David hit the tree. He tumbled off the cable car and landed in a heap in a pile of leaves.

I watched him in a cold sweat. "Move. Get up! Be okay."

Dad called down, "You okay, David? Shake it off boy!" David turned over on his back and examined a scrape on one of his arms. Relief flooded through me, making me feel warm and weak.

"That ain't nothing, Son," Dad called. "Rub some dirt on it."

David stood wobbly to his feet with his hands on his lower back. He leaned against the trunk for support and stretched from side to side. "I'm fine!" he shouted. Slowly, he staggered up the hill past us and went to the house.

Dad watched him a second before grabbing on to the rope. "So," he said, turning to the two of us, "whose next?"

"Uh, sorry Sir." Darrell rotated towards his house. "It's chore time." While Darrell was talking I edged away.

"Homework, Dad!" I called over my shoulder, before running inside.

*****

In the kitchen, Mom was comforting David. "I wish your dad would get a job instead of making those stupid toys." she muttered as she filled a dish towel with ice. "Everything he touches just turns to crap." She kissed him on the top of his head. "Hold that there a minute." Still clucking her tongue she hurried to hunt in the living room for her shoes. She only had a few minutes before she had to leave for the deli for her shift.

I looked over at David.

"You okay?"

He smiled, "Yeah, I'm fine." He gave me a thumbs-up. "Just knocked the air out of me. That was a cool ride until, you know, the end." We started snickering.

"Ever notice how Dad doesn't try out his inventions?" I asked.

He rolled his eyes.

Mom bumped past me to grab her keys off the table. "See you boys tonight." She patted my hand. "Keep an eye on Willie. There's pizza in the oven and broken cake in the Tupperware."

David and I gave each other a high five and sprinted for the yellow container at the end of the counter. I pried open the lid to reveal huge chunks of chocolate cake. Whenever a cake broke at work Mom brought it home for the Tupperware, and we'd eat it all week. We each grabbed a handful and stuffed them into our mouths, trying to make the grossest grin with brown-smeared teeth.

Our laughter woke Willie from his nap, and his little face peered over the railing at us. As soon as he saw the Tupperware, he crawled down the ladder calling for his share of the cake.

Dad walked in a couple hours later. "What are you little hooligans getting into in here? Trouble?"

David and Willie were playing Old Maid on the floor. I doodled in some spilled cake crumbs on the table.

"Jim, you don't look busy. Come on to town with me."

I jumped up and followed him outside, happy for time alone with Dad. I pulled opened the truck door and a bottle toppled out onto the ground at my feet. My heart dropped with it. Closing my eyes, I swallowed; please don't be there.

When I opened them it was still there. Dad was in the driver's seat lighting a cigarette and hadn't seen the bottle fall. I wasn't sure what to do with it. With the toe of my sneaker I nudged it under the truck.

I scrambled up into the truck seat as a knot formed in my stomach. How much had he drank? After taking a deep sniff, I thought maybe I could smell alcohol. I yanked my seatbelt across my lap and strapped it on, then bit my thumbnail.

"What were you looking at?" he asked, his eyes squinting from the smoke cloud around his head.

I shook my head and stared out the windshield. He shifted the truck into drive, and it purred like always, lurching forward down the driveway. Dad burped as we headed down the winding road back into town. I knew it, I did smelled alcohol.

We weren't on the road more than two minutes when headlights flashed in the rearview mirror. Dad cursed and flipped the mirror up as the lights blinded him. It was a little red coupe. I glanced in my side mirror and groaned.

"What a piece of crap," Dad growled. "What does he think, he owns the road?"

The driver drove right up on Dad's tail, maybe thinking he would pressure Dad into speeding up. Dad slammed on his brakes. The seatbelt locked around my waist as I jerked forward.

The red car's brakes screeched. It fishtailed side to side, but managed to stop without crashing in to the back of us.

Dad started again, but kept his speed even slower than before. The red car continued to tailgate us. My heart pounded, and I stared straight ahead, afraid to even glance in the side mirror again, and set Dad off.

Dad found a place on the shoulder and hauled the truck to the side to let the car pass. As the red car rocketed by Dad gave him the finger.

My chest loosened, and I took a deep breath. The problem had passed. Dad was letting him go around.

With a growl, Dad whipped the truck back on the road. He stepped on the gas until the engine roared. Our truck ate up the road until Dad was inches behind the red car.

I saw the guy's face peep into his rearview mirror. He looked scared. The red car sped up, taking the sharp corners at forty miles an hour trying to outrun us. Dad's big truck rode his bumper, threatening to ride right over the top and squash him like a pop can.

"You think you can tail-gate me," Dad sneered. His boozy breath hit me clear over by the window I was huddled against.

The car took a quick turn into the gas station. Dad swerved in behind him, jerked on the e-brake, and jumped out before the truck had a chance to come to a complete stop. The other guy was out of his car and backing away into the gas station, the palms of his hands up in front of him.

"You son of a bitch!" Dad clenched his fists. "You think you own the road. I'll show you who owns the road!"

"I'll call the cops!" the guy said. His face looked sickly and pale.

"I'll call the cops!" Dad mimicked back in a high, whiney voice. "You think I'm afraid of the cops?"

I wanted the man to run into the store. Dad had gotten into fist-fights for less than this. In my head I whispered, "Don't talk to him, turn and run away."

It's like the guy heard me, because he spun around and scuttled through the door.

The gas station owner poked his head out.

"What are you looking at?" Dad snarled at him. The owner shut the door quickly.

"That's right," Dad muttered. He climbed back into the still running truck, and gassed it hard, his eyebrows knotting together when we didn't move. "Oh," he murmured, and pushed down the e-brake.

He turned left on the road. I wondered if maybe he'd forgotten why we'd left in the first place, because he was driving back home. At the top of the driveway I hopped out as soon as he slowed down. Dad didn't get out, instead he threw the truck in reverse and backed away. Probably going to the bar, I thought, savagely. My time with Dad was ruined. I turned towards the house and saw the clear glass bottle sitting on the ground. In a fury, I kicked it as hard as I could. It spun a few times before it disappeared into the dark.

Chapter 9

November was a cold month. It was pitch black when I came down the ladder that morning. Dad was already awake and by the roaring woodstove. He was taking me hunting.

First, we drove to another house in one of the neighborhoods across town where we met up with Todd, one of dad's friends. Todd was a nerdy guy who worked in furniture sales, and Dad felt sorry for him. "You're thirteen, you've been hunting for years. But, he's never had a chance to hunt!" he'd told me with an incredulous tone the night before. Dad had set out to mend that.

We drove down to forest service land and parked the truck at the entrance of the road. Dad dragged the canoe from the bed, and we carried it on our shoulders out to the river. The snow was covered with an icy layer that crunched with each step.

It was freezing that morning. The horizon was a pale gray stripe high-lighting the black hills we were headed towards. Dad put the canoe in the river and held it steady with his hand. First Todd got in, groaning as he shifted his pack, then I climbed in, and finally Dad. He pushed us away from the shore with the oar and we leisurely floated away.

It was peaceful on the river. Birds were waking up around us, chirruping to let each other know it was morning and this was their territory. There weren't many that stuck around for the winter so their songs stuck out clear. The river rippled almost like a lullaby. I wanted to put my fingers in the water as the boat sliced through, but it was too cold. I rubbed the tops of my legs to warm them instead.

Dad put down the oar and grabbed his binoculars. He scanned the hillside for movement. A smile appeared on his lips and he held up one finger. I felt a tingle of excitement. Dad saw a deer.

Todd pulled his wool hat down further on his forehead and gave a little shiver.

"How are you liking it so far?" Dad asked. All of our talk was done in hush whispers.

"Dang cold out!" Todd rubbed his hands together.

Dad shook his head with a chuckle. "You just wait until we get out there. You'll warm up."

A few more paddles had the canoe bumping against the other side of the bank. Dad jumped out in his water proof-boots and held the boat steady in the water. I put my hand on his shoulder. It was as hard as a rock. I steadied myself and climbed out of the boat. After Todd was out, Dad dragged the boat up the bank.

We rested for a minute. Todd opened the thermos and passed around the steaming coffee. When it came to me I took a small sip, my lips automatically grimacing at the bitter taste. Then we slung our guns across our shoulders and were off.

The air was chilly, and the rising sun did nothing to dispel it. We trekked for miles through the silent woods, our feet leaving a trail in the snow. Dad found some fresh deer scat. He picked it up, rolled it between his fingers, and handed it to Todd. Todd squeezed it a few times before handing it back to me. I looked at it for a second before flinging it over my shoulder. What the heck was I going to do with it?

The forest had a special stillness that only seemed to happen when the temperature was below twenty degrees. My breath puffed in front of me white and thick. I felt like a dragon, and experimented with making cold smoke rings. I was bummed when it didn't work.

The deer had left the hill by the time we reached there. Todd's face fell when Dad said we needed to do some more tracking.

"How 'bout some food first? I'm starving."

Dad gave him a tight lipped grin, and waved me over so he could get into the backpack I carried. He pulled out some sandwiches and passed them around.

"Aren't we going to build a fire?" Todd asked, holding his wax papered sandwich in a limp hand.

"Well, we could, Todd, but we really need to keep going. We'll stay warm as long as we move."

Todd unwrapped the paper and took a bite of his sandwich. He looked like he was in pain that Dad wasn't going to build a fire.

"Ten minutes!" Dad said. "Eat 'em up."

We hiked for the rest of the afternoon, until Todd complained that his feet hurt. We never could find that deer again. It was a bitter pill not to have success, but the sun set kind of early up in the mountains, so we needed to head back.

Then Todd tripped and said he had to rest because he'd twisted his ankle. Dad gave a heavy sigh and looked at Todd as though he were sorry he'd brought him.

Todd wasn't moving. Dad rubbed his face and stamped his feet. "We've got to go. The truck's a long way back."

The temperature was dropping even more. Todd sighed and stood to his feet. He took a couple of slow steps.

"I don't want to be stuck trying to navigate the river in the dark," Dad warned.

It felt like forever trying to make it back to the river. Todd trudged the terrain like a three-legged turtle.

Once we arrived there, Dad held up his hands to make us pause. "Listen here, let me get the canoe in the water before you guys climb in. The canoe's kind of brittle. You step in it on a rock, you'll punch a hole right through."

Todd nodded. His face sagged from being exhausted.

Dad waded out into the river, pulling the canoe behind him. The other end was only a few inches in the water when Todd stepped into it.

Put his foot clear through the canoe.

Dad jerked at the sudden crunch. His mouth opened in shock. "Confound it Todd! Didn't you just hear me?"

It was dusk now, I could barely see either of their faces, let alone the other side of the river. I shivered.

Todd pulled his foot out with a little shake that splintered the fiberglass even more. He lost his balance and dropped the tackle bag into the river, where the current quickly snatched it. The bag held the rest of the food, but more importantly, the matches.

"Oh shoot!" Todd said, in a frantic voice. "I'm so sorry! So sorry!" The canoe started to fill with water.

Dad let out a stream of curse words that circled the three of us and echoed across the river.

"Just how the hell do you expect us to get back home now, Todd?" Dad said, before cussing again.

With a snarl, Dad yanked the boat into deeper water. "Give me your socks!" he demanded of Todd. Todd sat on the bank and peeled off his boots and socks. He threw the socks at Dad then replaced his boots. Dad balled the socks up and stuffed them in the hole.

"We've got one shot at this. Climb in, Todd. Start bailing with that thermos.

Dad helped me in. He shot Todd a dirty look as Todd grabbed the side and the boat rocked. Todd froze for a second, then carefully eased his foot into the boat. It sloshed in the water at the bottom.

"Hurry up! We don't have time for this." Dad blasted.

Todd gave Dad a nervous look and heaved the rest of himself on board.

"Keep that hole plugged!" Dad yelled as he climbed on board. He threw an oar into the water and started to paddle.

Todd pressed his boot over the socks forcing them down in the hole. There were already two inches of water in the canoe. Dad looked at it bitterly. There was nothing to be done. We had to get out of the river before we sunk.

Todd bailed the water out as fast as he could with the thermos. The water crept higher and higher up my legs. My heart beat like a woodpecker inside my chest. I started throwing water out with my hands. By the time we were in the middle of the river it had already filled the boat with four inches.

My hands were so cold, like blocks of ice. I couldn't control my shivering. Dad was rowing like a wild man. I was rooting for him. "Go faster! Go faster!"

At about five feet from shore Dad scrambled out and pulled the boat the rest of the way to the bank. I grabbed my gun and climbed after him. He threw me the keys and said, "Go start the truck and get the heat going."

He left Todd to get out by himself.

I darted down the trail. It was dark, and the wind was already icing up my wet pants. When I saw the truck on the side of the road I nearly cried, I was so darn happy. Climbing inside, I turned the key and slid the heat on to maximum blast, holding my frozen hands in front of the vent.

The men tossed the canoe into the back and climbed in the cab. We were all shivering, our teeth chattering. Todd never said a word. I didn't blame him.

About an hour later, we dropped Todd off at his house. Before he shut the car door he leaned in, "Can I just say one more time how sorry I am?"

Dad put the truck in reverse, and it did a little jerk. "Yeah, don't worry about it."

Todd nodded and slammed the door. Somehow, I didn't think I'd ever see him in the woods again.

Dad and I listened to the radio on the way home. The heat was on full force, and it burned my face but still hadn't touched the chilled-to-the-bone feeling I had going on inside.

Dad was doing some weird sing-song mumbling. I shot him a quick glance. He was singing, "Karma, karma, karma, karma, karma Chameleon," making me burst out in laughter when I recognized it. Dad continued to bob his head to the beat. "What?" he asked. "It's Culture Club. Haven't you heard of them before?" He continued to bob. "I like this song."

"Dad, you're not serious. Everyone knows this song."

Just before our driveway Dad turned the radio down.

"Hey, you did real good out there," he said. I smiled inside. Simple words but they made every bit of the freezing cold worth it.

He idled at the top of the driveway. The moonlight shone through the windshield and across one side of his face. He shifted the truck into reverse. "You go on in and warm up. Bring the guns. I'm going to go out and unwind for a while."

*****

That night we were all woken by a loud thump. Dad had come home drunk and hungry. He crashed through the kitchen for a while. I listened, worried that things were about to be thrown and broken. Instead I heard loud gags. Dad had apparently been hungry and grabbed a handful of cake crumbs from the Tupperware, only to spit it out. Mom had left another container there on the counter filled with manure for the greenhouse.

She laughed and laughed.

Chapter 10

I crouched behind the loft railing with a BB gun balanced against the rail. David was hiding somewhere in the living room down below.

PING! A BB hit my helmet. I fired back in response then began to pump the air rifle for another volley. It only took two good pumps to make the BB mean business when it made contact. David's helmet surfaced from behind the back of the couch like an empty turtle shell. I lined up the BB gun for the shot. Carefully, as my breath hissed out, I pulled the trigger. David dove to the side. Just missed him! He aimed back.

SNAP!

"Dude!" I jumped up, cupping my eye. "You fricking got my eye!"

David froze for a second, unsure if I was faking or not. "You okay?" He ran across the living room and hurried up the ladder.

It didn't feel like the eyeball. I leaned forward and flicked at the corner of my eye. The BB fell out of my lid and hit a plywood board with a rat-tat-tat-tat. I looked up at the ceiling and winked my eye. "Yeah, I'm fine." I said, blinking a few times. Blood started to drip down my cheek in red tears. I grabbed a shirt off the floor and wiped it.

"That was an awesome shot!"

We gave each other a high-five.

I was fourteen, and after a brief semester in middle school, this was my brothers' and my first week back to being homeschooled again. I'd originally returned to public school because I missed my friends, but Mom pulled us out after a long discussion with one of her friends about the evils of the school system. In the end, David and I didn't mind. It meant a break from the gossip of the kids talking about all the times Dad got pulled over for DUI's.

And, of course, it meant freedom again.

Dad didn't have much say about our schooling one way or another. Little by little, he was fading into the background because of the alcohol. It had been a rough year. I think he felt like everyone in the house had chosen a side, and it wasn't his.

I tried to take things into my own hands to keep them from fighting. I figured if I kept the kitchen spotless then Mom wouldn't yell at Dad for being lazy. All throughout the school year, as soon as I got home from the bus, I started cleaning.

I still kept the same schedule since being homeschooled again. Holding the t-shirt to my face, I squinted at the clock by my bed. It was time to start. I wiped the blood one more time and headed down the ladder.

"You going to help me clean?" I called up to David as I walked into the kitchen.

"You know that never helps." David yelled back.

"Whatever," I muttered. Cleaning helped, cleaning was important. I had to do something. In some ways, I felt like I was the guy that had to bridge the gap between them, the peace maker. I was the one that helped them stay together.

I started on the counter, loading the sink with dishes, and wiping as I went. When I got to the sink, I washed and dried the dishes. Then I swept the kitchen, down the hall and into the bathroom. I gave everything in the bathroom a quick once-over and then swept the living room.

It was sparkling by the time I was done.

Dad came home first, from a handy-man job he'd been offered by Mom's friend at church. He went to the Tupperware and helped himself to a big handful of cake.

"Howdy boys," he waved a hand at us. "Where's Willie?"

"At Grandma's," I said, staring at the crumbs on the counter. He walked over to the fridge and found a beer, cracking it open on the way to his easy chair. After flipping on the TV, he adjusted the tin foil swathed coat-hanger we used as an antenna until Star Trek came in clear. Then, he settled into his chair with a heavy sigh.

I watched him from the corner of the kitchen, and something hurt inside. I wanted my dad to be the hero I saw him as when I was a little boy. Not some man everyone called a drunkard, getting charity work from church.

I know he tried. He still aimed to do his best by us. Just last month he came to our rescue with the neighbor man who'd kept pestering us boys to come watch a movie with him in his camper. Dad heard about it and went up there with a tire iron. I don't know what happened, but the guy never bothered me or my brothers again, not so much as a look in our direction. Later, there were whispers in the neighborhood that the man was a creeper.

Dad put his feet up and gave a chuckle at something Bones said. I walked back to the counter and brushed the cake crumbs into my hand, flicking them into the garbage.

David whistled in the loft. He'd stay up there until Mom came home, and she was due any minute.

Sure enough, I heard the rattle screech of her car driving up to the house. Dad closed his eyes and let out a quiet groan. There was a delay, maybe Mom getting out some groceries, before both of the car doors slammed. A second later Willie burst through the front door.

He skidded through the kitchen to the cake Tupperware. "Hi Dad!"

"Hi yourself," Dad answered, tipping the beer can up at him.

Mom came in through the open door, her arms filled with groceries.

"Why doesn't anyone help me?" she asked from behind the bags.

"Coming Mom!" David hollered from the loft, and slid down the ladder.

She walked into the kitchen and set down the bags.

"Oh my word! Look at this mess," she glared, the two wrinkles now scarred into permanent lines between her eyebrows.

I flipped my head to look. There were more cake crumbs on the counter. Willie bit his lip and backed up. A heavy weight grew inside my chest.

She turned to Dad. "All you do is sit here on your ass all day doing nothing! Leaving everything for me to do when I come home!" She grabbed a dish towel and wiped the counter, and then brushed off her hands. "I'm working myself to the bone here." She threw the towel down. "I guess I have to make dinner now." She wrenched a pan out of the cupboard and slammed it on the stove. "Jim, come over here."

I eased my way to the kitchen and stood behind her, every fiber wanting to run away.

"So," she smiled, "How was your day."

"Good." I swallowed.

"How long has Dad been home?" She indicated him with the spatula.

"Not long."

"Long enough to get a beer though."

"I can hear you, Woman!" Dad yelled from his chair.

I backed away as she turned to argue, and managed to sneak out through the still open door into the front yard. My brothers were already there.

"Think we're going to Grandma's tonight?" David asked, tossing a pebble back and forth between his hands.

I shrugged. Four times this past year Mom had taken us to Grandma's house. On the way there, Mom would tell us what a bum Dad was. Her voice was burned in my head, "Everything he touches turns to crap."

I hated how I felt inside; worried, confused, angry. Alone.

I shook my head. "C'mon, let's get out of here." It was the only thing left I could do, get my brothers away.

*****

The next Sunday morning, Mom flew around the house trying to get all of us ready. Dad was already out in his tool shed working on who knew what. He didn't go to church with us anymore. Everyone there knew my parents had problems.

When we got to church Mom walked down the aisle to her friends. The women huddled around the front pew to chat for a few minutes before the opening chords of the organ signaled that everyone better be seated. My brothers and I hung around the back waiting for other kids to show up.

One of the men in the foyer ambled up to me. He was friends with my mom but I hardly knew him.

"Hi Jim. How are you?" He paused for a second, his eyebrows turned down in sad commas. "How's your dad?"

A lump started in my throat. I knew what he was asking. "Good," I muttered, looking passed him for an escape. He put his hand on my shoulder and smiled down sympathetically. Pityingly. My insides pulled up tight.

Then, heat started to build inside of me.

I spun away from him and hid in the bathroom. I was shaking inside. Why was Dad doing this to us? Everyone was talking about us.

Church extended later than usual. That afternoon, when we came home, Dad was sitting in the front yard with the lawn mower. As we pulled up in the driveway he glanced up, then back down at the engine again. He held a brown bottle to his lips and took a drink. He looked small, like half the man he used to be.

I slammed the car door shut and started for the house.

"C'mere boy," he called to me. "Help me with this thing."

I groaned inside and walked towards him.

There were several parts of the engine strewn across the grass. He held one of the greasy parts close to his face, trying to focus. His eyes were tired when they flicked over at me.

"How's church?

I shrugged. "It's okay."

"Yeah, church." Dad shook his head and sighed. "All my friends there've turned their backs on me."

I picked at a leaf, not knowing what to say.

He took another drink. "That's okay. I've got friends of my own."

I swallowed the lump in my throat.

He took another swallow and studied me again. "You know, I worry about you. Out of all my boys, you're the most like me."

I nodded. Mom told me that too, whenever she was mad at me.

He tapped the carburetor with his screwdriver to knock off the rust. Then he grabbed the carb cleaner and sprayed the port. I dug the screws out of the dirt and handed them to him. He grabbed them with his calloused fingers and screwed the lid back on.

"Well, that's good, I think that's good," he mumbled. "Go ahead and give that cord a pull."

I stood up and gave it a yank, and the motor sprung to life for a few seconds, before dying again.

"Crap," he said, and started to pull apart the spark plug assembly.

As he worked, he began to talk about his army days, days when he was still a hero. I could feel a part of me thaw. He smiled at me, and I smiled back. He shared a story about how he and his army buddies snuck the military jeep out for a night, and we both laughed.

He screwed the spark plug back in.

"Try it again, Son."

I pulled the cord again. The lawn mower still wouldn't start.

Dad stood there frozen for a moment, and something changed in the air.

He clenched his fist. Then, leapt up cussing, the bottle of beer flung to the side, forgotten. His face was furious and red, the look telling me, "I'm going to rip this cussed lawn-mower apart, and anybody else who gets in my way."

Somehow, I'd woken the giant, and I wanted to crawl under a rock and hide.

Instead, I backed away and left him kicking the lawn-mower and hurried inside the house.

"What's going on out there?" Mom asked while mixing raw hamburger meat. Her hands were covered with bits of seasoning and goo.

"Nothing," I said.

Outside, we could hear Dad screaming. There was a loud crash when he swung the wrench against the lawn mower. Then silence.

He was coming inside.

The door slammed open. Dad walked over to the sink for a glass of water.

"You're going to shock your body drinking something that isn't alcohol." Mom said.

"Don't start with me, Woman!" Dad snarled.

And from there, it was on. I sighed, as they traded shots back and forth about her disappointment, his failures, and his defensive come-backs.

I ran out to the woods to find my brothers. I figured they were probably hiding in the tree house. Instead, they were out by the old car. This past summer, we'd tried to figure out what was wrong with it, lifting the hood and examining the engine. The hood was still up, exposing a V-8, all covered in rust.

David and Willie sat with their BB guns across their knees. I walked up just in time to overhear, "Get him in the shoulder." There were snickers, and then I felt the sharp sting of a BB splat into my shirt.

"You little creeps!" I yelled.

David lay back on the cracked, vinyl seat. "I didn't do it," he said innocently. Willie laughed but pointed the gun at me to warn me off.

"I'll get ya back later," I muttered.

"You get him, and I'm telling," David said.

"Shut up, or I'll roll you down the driveway again."

David punched me in the shoulder. He hadn't cared for the trip he took last summer down the driveway in the old fifty gallon drum.

We heard shouts from the house.

"How's it going in there?" David asked.

I kicked at a rock, trying to hit the rim of the tire. "The usual. Maybe we should head down to Elias and Ruby's to get some food."

David nodded, and the three of us started down the path.

Just then we heard the front door slam, and then a squeal of tires of Dad's truck.

Then, Mom yelled out for us. "Boys! Boys!"

Willie wrinkled his forehead. I felt the steam leave me too. Visions of Ruby's home-made chocolate chip cookies evaporated in a dark cloud.

She was waiting on the stoop when we broke free of the woods. As soon as she saw us she called, "Go get your back packs! We're out of here!"

We slowly climbed up the ladder to the loft. I pulled my already packed back-pack off of the headboard post. Mom was talking to herself down stairs.

"I'm not taking this anymore! I'm done! Done! Done! Done!"

She hustled us outside and into her car without even bothering to lock the front door.

Instead of getting on the highway for Grandma's she turned the car towards town.

"Where are we going?" I asked.

She shifted her car, and it gave a lurch before going into gear. "I called Chloe, and she invited us to come stay with her." Chloe was Mom's church friend. "She honestly doesn't see how I've dealt all these years with your father." The car lurched again.

I thought about how adamant she'd been when we left the house.

I don't think even she knew how done she was.

Chapter 11

Mom sped up into Chloe's driveway and parked the car, where it shuddered a few times before the engine shut off. The four of us piled out, hauling our back packs after us. The porch light flipped on as we closed the car door, and Chloe came out onto the porch with her arms crossed to wait.

"I just can't deal with this anymore." Mom frowned.

"Oh my goodness," Chloe said. "Well, come in everyone! Come in."

We filed into her house one by one. Mom set her stuff on the couch while the three of us boys stood awkwardly against the living room wall. There was one lamp on, and I was glad it was dark. I felt kind of embarrassed for bursting in like some homeless refugee.

"Make yourself at home. Sit down wherever." Chloe fluttered around in green slippers. "Have you eaten?"

Mom sighed. "I was just putting the meatloaf in the oven when he started in."

"Oh dear."

"Yes, you remember what I was telling you earlier? He's always the same."

"You poor thing," Chloe clucked her tongue. "All right then. Well, let's see what I have."

Chloe disappeared into the kitchen. The fridge door opened. There was a long pause, then we heard clinks of jars and containers being pushed around. It sounded like a desperate hope that something would materialize behind the jars that would feed three boys.

It didn't sound too promising though, because then the fridge shut and the cupboard doors clattered.

My brothers and I trooped like robots over to the couch and sat. David smacked my knee with his, staring straight ahead like he didn't do nothing. I bumped him back harder.

Chloe reappeared in the doorway. "Okay, how's peanut butter and jelly sandwiches sound?" She gave a little laugh. "I guess I need to go shopping."

"That's fine, that's good," Mom said reassuringly. "We don't want to put you out."

"Oh, it's no trouble." Chloe went back into the kitchen. This time Mom followed.

Their voices were low, but I could hear them talking. We stayed quiet in the living room all wishing, I think, that we were back in our woods. A few minutes later they both came out with plates of peanut butter and jelly sandwiches.

"I know how boys like to eat," Chloe said with a nod in our direction.

Peanut butter and jelly was my least favorite food ever, but Mom gave me a glare behind Chloe's back. I picked one up and held it tentatively. Grape jelly oozed out of the side.

"Mmm," I took a bite. "So good!"

My brothers grabbed one too. Willie licked up one edge of his sandwich.

Chloe snapped the TV set on and turned it to Wheel of Fortune. My brothers and I stared uninterested, while Mom and Chloe shouted out guesses to the contestants.

"You know they can't hear you, right Mom?" Willie said.

"Oh shush. You know we're just having fun," Mom said.

Just then the phone rang.

It was Dad. How he knew where we were, I had no idea.

"My son's think I'm a bad man," he said, his voice so loud I could hear it from where I was sitting. "Maybe I am!"

David jumped up and grabbed the phone from Mom. "Dad! Knock it off! Leave us alone!"

"You think I'm a bad man," Dad mumbled.

"Just leave us be, Dad."

"I'm coming up there, and I'm going to let you beat me up." Dad slurred.

"No Dad, leave us alone. You're drunk."

"You can hit me."

"Dad, if you go anywhere, I'm calling the cops and reporting you drinking and driving."

Dad started to laugh, or maybe cry, I couldn't tell. David slammed the phone down, shaking.

I sat like a statue.

David punched the wall, then ripped the phone back off the receiver.

"I'm sick of this." His chin jutted forward. "I'm not putting up with it anymore." He pressed the buttons for the police.

I understood David's frustration. I was frustrated too.

When the operator answered, David blurted out, "My dad's drunk. He said he was coming up here. He's drunk driving right this minute."

Now, the police had been involved many times in my parents' disputes. So much so, that they knew my dad by his first name. They knew all his haunts and knew how combative he was when he was drunk. When he was plastered he wasn't afraid of the police or anybody else who got in his way. He didn't have any problem knocking a person down.

David started to pace, as he listened to the other end.

"No, he got rid of the yellow Toyota last week. He's got a new truck, now. It's white." The telephone cord stretched taut as he came to the end of his tether. Abruptly, he spun around and paced back. "Yes. Okay, Okay, thank you."

David hung up the phone, looking down confused at how the cord was tangled around his body. He rotated a few times to release himself.

We all watched him like a knot of owls sitting on a fence.

"They're going to call back if they find him."

Small town police work like that.

Mom patted David on the arm when he squished into the couch next to her. "You're such a brave boy." She studied him for a second. "I'm sorry he's doing this to you. To all of you." She sighed and clicked the TV volume back up.

Pat Sajak was congratulating the contestant on guessing the phrase, "Rubber Baby Buggy Bumpers." None of us spoke. The plate of sandwiches on the coffee table looked lifeless, and the air felt prickly and unnatural. I wondered where Dad was and what was going to happen next.

The phone rang again. We all jumped at the jarring tone. Mom looked at my brother, then me; which one of us was going to pick it up?

I walked across the narrow living room to the phone and cleared my throat. "H..hello?"

"This is Officer Palomo. We have a unit who's located your dad, and they're in pursuit. We'll have him in custody soon."

"Okay, thank you." I tried to make my voice sound deep and manly, but it hurt to speak over the lump in my throat. Slowly, I put the phone back in the cradle and turned to look at the family.

"They've found him. They're chasing him right now."

The room came alive with nervous energy. Everyone talked at once.

"Where is he at?"

"Is he coming here?"

"Leave it to your father to cause a road chase." Mom spoke over the top of all of us. She sounded exasperated.

A vivid picture flashed through my mind of Dad drunk and losing control of the truck on a sharp turn and hitting a tree. A ball of flames. I ground my palms into my eyes. Please God, make this stop!

"I hope they catch him!" David's eyes shone bright with anger. I nodded. My youngest brother grabbed another sandwich and sat eating it by the window.

Chloe stood by Mom. "It's just a shame this happened." She patted my mom's arm. Mom's eyes were squeezed tight, wet, and her lips twisted into a trembling frown. She sniffed, then looked for my little brother.

"Willie! Come here, honey," she called to him. Willie ignored her.

"Willie!"

"Leave me alone," he said, "I want to sit here." The curtain draped across his shoulders like a cape as he looked out the window.

Mom watched him for a minute, biting her lip.

"If he only knew what he was doing to his boys," she spoke softly to Chloe. We all heard her.

He had to know what he was doing, I thought.

The phone rang again. We stared at it like it was on fire. This time Mom went to answer it.

"Hello," she paused. "Yes, this is Pearl." She twirled to face us. "What? You can't be serious. He escaped?"

There was droning on the other end for a minute, while Mom sank to the couch with her mouth hanging open.

"Okay, thank you for letting us know." She got up and walked back to the wall receiver and hung up the phone. Turning toward us, she said, "They said he got away from them. Somehow, they lost him in a field of corn." Her eyes creased with worry. "He has a rifle in the back seat. They told us to be careful; he might be on his way here."

I jumped up. My arms and legs tingled, and I spun in a circle, not sure of what to do or where to go.

That electrified Mom. "Quick! Turn out the lights!" she yelled. We raced around the house flipping the light switches off. I heard "Ow!" in the dark hallway as my two brothers careened into each other.

When the lights were all out we gathered back together in the living room. Chloe flipped off the TV. The thick darkness wrapped us as though it had real weight. We stumbled through it to our spots on the couch.

My brothers sat together and whispered back and forth. My heart was about to beat out of my chest. I wondered if they could hear it.

The open window brought no relief. It was pitch black even outside. Up the block the orange street lamp flickered, and then snapped out. Even the moon had given up its fight against the overcast sky.

Silently, I prayed. Don't look for us, Dad. Get away from here!

I heard the roar of his truck burning up the road before anyone else did. The sound hit me like a knife. His headlights splashed against the back wall of the living room, making a macabre shadow puppet show as we ducked down out of sight of the windows. The truck's tires spit up Chloe's gravel driveway when he skidded to a stop.

The heavy door slammed. I held my breath, I think we all did.

His footsteps crunched through the gravel and thumped up to the front door.

Then nothing.

My pulse beat double time in my throat.

In the distance a dog barked.

BAMBAMBAMBAMBAM! The door shook as he beat against it in fury. We all jumped. Mom squealed, and then muffled her mouth with her hand.

"Pearl! I know you're in there!"

My breath rushed in and out like I'd just raced up a mountain. Willie scuttled over to be close to me. I patted him on the head.

"Shhh," I whispered into the top of his head. "It's gonna be okay."

BAMBAMBAMBAM! Dad pounded on the door again. Around the neighborhood porch lights flicked on. Now we could see him out there.

A rifle was in his hands.

"Dammit! I know you're in there! Come out! You think I'm a piece of crap! Get out here now!" We could hear his breathing on the other side of the door. Deep breaths, then a cough.

"Hell no." he muttered. "You ain't going to ignore me tonight." We heard more crunching as he walked away.

Mom straightened a little to take a quick peek outside. Her head bobbed as she looked one way, and then the other. "Where'd he go?" she hissed.

The adrenaline was making me shake. I squeezed my hands into fists to keep them still.

Then we heard the brittle smash of glass breaking. Mom peeked again.

"Oh my word! Your father's kicking out the headlights of my car!" In the glow from the porch light I could see Mom shiver. I scurried around the furniture to the window and sat up on my heels to watch him from below the window sill. There was a metallic crash when he threw back the hood of her blue Datsun. He leaned over and messed with something deep in the engine. He gave a mighty jerk. When he stood up a bunch of ripped out wires dangled from his hand like old dandelion stems. He flung them to the ground.

Mom crept to the phone. She pulled it down to the floor and dialed the police.

"He's here," she said in a furious tone. "He's outside right now! Where are you?" There was a pause.

"Yes, I'll stay on." she put her hand over the mouth piece. "They said they've already sent police here, and they're just up the road."

It wasn't but a half a minute later that we heard the police car's sirens blaring. Dad ran for his truck, scrambling in his coat pocket for his keys. Three police cars turned down the road. Dad revved his truck up, reversed hard, and sped away. Two police cars followed him. The chase was on again.

The last police car pulled into the driveway. The siren flipped off, but the lights still flashed their strobe pattern. Mom walked outside to greet them, the colors splashing across her face and body.

I followed right behind. Along the street doors popped open one by one, with nosy neighbors coming out to gawk at us. I cringed and went back into the house, ramming into David on the way.

"What's with you?" he asked

"Everyone's staring at us!"

David didn't say anything, just watched me for a moment before going out to Mom. I sat alone in the dark living room with my head in my hands. I wanted to run away from my whole crazy family.

The squeal of tires forced me to look up again. I hurried outside just in time to see Dad backing down the road towards the police in the driveway. He parked the truck and sat there with his hands held out the window.

The police man rocketed away from Mom and pulled his gun from the holster. He cautiously walked closer. "Get out of the truck!" the cop yelled. "Keep your hands where I can see them."

Just then the other two cop cars came flying down the road. They screeched to a stop behind Dad's truck.

Dad cracked open the truck door. He looked straight to the porch, straight at me, and his eyes bore into mine. I saw shame and regret. My heart ached and I had to look away, feeling like I had betrayed him. Family is supposed to protect family, not let them get hauled away by the police, even when they deserve it.

"Get on the ground! Get on the ground!" the cops yelled. Dad dropped down to his knees when the cops rushed him.

They grabbed Dad by the arms and threw him up against the side of the truck. His body made a loud smack when it hit the vehicle, and he cried out when they sharply twisted his arms behind his back to cuff him. Then, they dragged him to the cop car.

Dad wouldn't look at me again as they drove away.

I watched the fading tail lights of the cop car take my dad, and the dark silhouettes of the neighbors talking to one another. One of them had a phone to his head as he stood on his porch.

In that instant something inside of me snapped. I wasn't going to let him do this to me anymore. I wasn't going to feel guilty about not taking his side. I was done taking sides, unless it was mine.

Chapter 12

It was the next Monday at noon that Dad was released from jail. Mom's co-worker, Betty, lived across from the jail house, and had called to give her the heads up.

We lived in a good ol' town and a gun charge never came up against him. Instead, Dad was cited with yet another indictment of driving under the influence. He'd already been hauled to jail so many times through the years for DUI's that he was on first name basis with the jailers.

He went back to our home on the hill. But this time we weren't there.

Years later, when I look back at my childhood I believe this was the point when my dad gave up. I think part of him died when we weren't there. He'd known he'd gone too far, and lost any hope to be able to fix it. He just didn't want to try any more.

During that time we continued to live at Chloe's. It was a little crazy in her house. I claimed the long couch, which meant my brother had to sleep curled up on the love seat. Willie had a sleeping bag on the floor. Every morning it was a fight for the bathroom since Chloe didn't feel quite as free as Mom did about us boys going outside.

Later that month, I went back with Mom to the house on the hill. We'd had word from the neighbor that the coast was clear, and with Dad gone, Mom wanted to pack up some of our stuff.

My muscles felt tight as we rattled up the driveway. We pulled up to the top, and I could see for myself that Dad's truck wasn't there and gave a deep exhale. I hadn't realized I'd been holding my breath. But, I still wanted to hurry and get the heck out of there in case he came home.

Mom fiddled with her keys to unlock the door, but it opened the moment she touched it. As we walked in the house a gust of wind banged the door behind us.

The hair on my neck stood up. The house didn't smell right, didn't feel right.

It only took about two more steps to see the carnage. Glass lay sprayed across the concrete floor, crunching under my sneakers as I eased over to the kitchen. Next to the kitchen table rested a rusty wheelbarrow, flipped upside down. The kitchen window was just a frame with sharp jags of broken glass after the wheelbarrow had been chucked through.

The refrigerator door was wide open. Its light was on and it smelled like hot rubber from running non-stop. Plastic shelves inside were knocked askew, and the bottom half of the fridge was filled with sand. There was so much that it had spilled out into a pile on the floor. The vibrations of my steps made even more trickle out.

"Oh my word, Jim. Look at this."

Trying to be watchful of the glass, I spun to look. Mom pointed to the wall opposite the kitchen. It was covered in slabs of something pinkish brown. I edged across the floor carefully to investigate. Dad had thrown hotdogs so hard that they'd exploded and stuck to the plaster.

I could imagine the look on Dad's face when he threw them. Red fury.

I was stunned, surrounded by the evidence that Dad had given up on his family. Dad had been so proud of the house he'd built, even if it originally had been a garage. Every action screamed, "Screw you!"

The smell of smoke drifted through the broken window. I opened the back door to look. Smudgy embers still burned in the skeleton ashes of an old bonfire in the back yard.

My stomach churned with bile. I didn't want to know what Dad had burned.

Mom pushed passed me with her lips pursed tight. She snatched a stick up from the wood pile and marched over to the fire. Sifting through the ashes she flipped out a charred red corner of a book with the tip of the stick.

Our family photo album.

"Oh my gosh! How could he do that? How could he?" She stirred the ashes with frantic motions scattering the embers, but there was nothing more in there. I had to look away before her tears came.

Our photos, gone. I'd never felt such a loss, so broken, and yes, steaming anger.

I grabbed on to the anger as soon as I sensed it. It was a relief. Anger made me strong. This is what the love of a father looked like? Embarrassment, humiliation, fear, destroying everything I cared about? Well, screw him too.

Anger made me not a victim.

I walked out to the fire and put my arm around Mom's shoulder.

"Come on, Mom. Let's go get our stuff and get out of here." She rolled in to me and started to cry. I patted her back. "It's okay, Mom. We've got this. We're going to be okay." After a minute, she snuffled into a corner of her sweater and then gave me a wet face smile. My shirt was damp from where she'd rested her head.

We packed up two suitcases and headed back to Chloe's. We didn't tell my brothers what had happened at the house. I didn't talk about Dad at all, never wanted to again. I wasn't going to think about Dad after all he did to us.

I didn't need a father. I was almost fifteen, I guess I was old enough to take care of myself. How much worse could I possibly do?

Chapter 13

"Hey Ma! Where's my socks?" I dug through my duffel bag looking for my clothes.

"I don't know. Check the laundry basket!" Mom called from Chloe's kitchen. She was packing lunches for us. We'd been at Chloe's for a few months now. After everything going on with her work, and our living arrangements, my butt was back in public school as a sophomore.

I walked down the hall to the laundry room, bumping into David on the way. Already, a change was happening, and we weren't seeing much of each other anymore. It's like my parents split had cracked the bond between all of us.

David had a toothbrush in his mouth as he waited for his turn in the bathroom.

"Hey!" I yelled. "That's my Stryper t-shirt!"

"I found it in my pile." David shrugged at me. "Mine now."

"Aww this is bull crap. You have my socks on too?"

"If they're in my pile, they're mine." He pushed past me and banged on the bathroom door. "Hurry up, Willie! You can't take all day!"

I flipped on the laundry room light. The wicker basket sitting on the washing machine had already been dug through. What was left was Mom's shirts, a couple dish towels, and a twisted pair of blue jeans. No socks.

"Hurry up boys! The bus is coming!"

I slammed the top of the washing machine with my palm. Great, day old socks, I felt like a scum bag. I could already tell it was going to be a horrible day.

*****

I hated school. I tapped my pencil against the side of my notebook and watched the clock, just waiting for class to end so I could get a cigarette. Earlier that morning one of the teachers had patted my arm and asked me about Dad. Made me sick. What was I supposed to say? Yeah he's a drunk. Mom and Dad are getting a divorce and I heard he has a girlfriend now. Even though it was old news, people still talked about his drunken night on the town. Screw them. I didn't care anymore.

I was just here at school to do the time so I could graduate. Still two years left to go, though. Felt like an eternity.

A balled up piece of paper hit me on the back of my neck. I glanced back and Thomas waved at me with a goofy grin on his face. We'd met my first day in mechanics class, and had been good friends ever since. We also worked together in the kitchen of the local truck stop. I examined him now. His curly hair looked like a mess of dandelion fluff on top of his head. I had to laugh.

"What?" I asked him.

"We have a new kid to initiate tonight," Thomas said. I arched my eyebrow.

He jerked his thumb in the direction of a scrawny kid sitting two rows away. I nodded in the kid's direction.

"Him?"

"He just got a job as a dishwasher."

Ahhh, I smiled, then straightened back in the seat. Anticipating tonight's fun was a good distraction.

When the final bell rang I threw my books in my locker and hurried outside. I didn't care about homework. I'd worry about that tomorrow. Thomas was already waiting for me in his black GTO. We'd spent hours after school and on the weekend restoring that car. It purred like a kitten. He took off as soon as I jumped into the passenger seat, roasting the tires and leaving two black stripes in the parking lot.

I rolled the window down and stuck my head out into the wind. The spring sun was hot on my face. "WOOOOHOOOOOO!"

We squirreled around a bit on some back roads, then drove to an empty church parking lot and spun donuts. Afterwards, we headed to work.

Truck Depot was a dive that all the truckers loved. The restaurant did have a mean breakfast buffet, as long as you avoided the biscuits and gravy. I had no idea what the gravy was. It looked like astronaut food and came in powder form in a can, before we hit it with boiling water to make it gel up. Anyway, the dinner crowd was already in, all rowdy and wanting their hamburgers and fried chicken with a side of steak fries.

We went through the restaurant to the back where the kitchen was. The sinks were overflowing with pyramids of crusty plates, pots, and cups sitting in grey water. The new kid stood next to the counter, being trained. He looked nervous, dressed in a clean white apron, his bony arms dangling by his side. Thomas elbowed me and we both snickered. We knew the apron wouldn't be clean for long.

When Alice, the head cook, saw us she waved us over. She said to the kid, "I'm turning you over to these guys." Then, jabbing her thumb in the direction of the kid, "This is Eric." Pointing at us, "This is Thomas and Jim. Don't let them push you around." With that she gave us a wink and walked to the double burners on the other side of the kitchen where hamburger fat was spitting.

Eric nodded at us. "Hey."

We nodded back. I wandered over to the sink, waving for him to follow along. Together, Eric and I sprayed down and washed the racks of dishes, while Thomas scraped the plates. I watched Thomas out of the corner of my eye. He was surreptitiously removing the little unused pats of butter from the plates and set them out of sight. We worked for a few hours and pretty much busted our butts keeping up with the dishes. It was hot in the kitchen, with only one grime covered fan spinning lazily in the corner, and soon sweat was trickling down our backs and making our hair wet.

Finally, Alice told us we could take a break.

Eric, Thomas, and I got cherry sodas at the fountain and went outside behind the restaurant. Leaning against the brick wall, I lit a cigarette.

"So," Eric bit his fingernail off and spat it, "you guys finish your economics homework?"

I laughed. "Not even close. You?"

"Naw, I'll get my sister to do it tonight."

"What?" Thomas took a swig of his soda. "Your sister does your homework?"

"Yeah she does. If she wants me to take her to the parties, she'd better."

"Cool! Maybe she should do mine. I'll take her to a party." Thomas gave a half smile.

Eric shook his head, but smiled. "Man, just shut up."

We joked around some more. Eric was pretty cool.

Alice stuck her head out the metal door. "Dishes piling up in here," she warned.

I stubbed out my cigarette against the wall. Eric stepped on his and then he followed us back inside.

Eric did pretty well with keeping up with the dishes, so I left him to go tackle the pans. They were older than dirt and had to be handled carefully because their rough edges would slice through skin, leaving it gaping wide and bloody. It wasn't easy washing dishes with a bloody hand, I ought to know.

I glanced over at Thomas. He was squeezing the butter packs one by one into his hand. He looked up at me and gave a silent laugh. Gently, he molded the butter into a baseball. Then, just like he was bowling, he lined up with his target, Eric's back end as he leaned over the sink. Thomas took a wind up, then let the butter fly. I held my breath as it sailed through the air. It splatted up between Eric's legs. I laughed so hard I could barely stand, and staggered against the sink. Eric looked down, confused, then set after us with the water hose.

Alice yelled from her corner. "Hey! What's going on over there?" We didn't answer, just laughed harder. Good times.

Chapter 14

The months added up, until we'd been at Chloe's for over a year. Mom had been using the time to go back to school and earn a degree. I'd just turned sixteen when Mom was able to get a job that paid more than the deli and we moved out to a studio apartment. We didn't have much to move, which was probably a good thing. The room was small and heated up like a toaster oven with the four of us in it.

After all those years of freedom in the woods, I dreaded going home to the studio after school. It always felt like the four walls were closing in on me, and there was no place to just sit and be quiet. Even if I was the only one home, which rarely happened, it didn't feel quiet because of all the school books, clothing, towels and dishes that spilled over and onto every square inch.

That night, after work, Thomas drove me to the studio. I frowned when I looked up at our window. The lights were off. My brothers would be asleep on the bunk beds. I was supposed to have a bunk bed too, but usually crashed on the couch rather climb on the bottom bunk that squeaked all night every time my brother moved.

Thomas must have seen me hesitate before opening the car door. "You want to just crash at my house? We've got that loft above the garage," he said. It didn't take me but two seconds for my brain to comprehend his words.

"Hell yes!" I answered.

From then on, I stayed in the loft at Thomas' house every chance I got.

The longer I stayed at Thomas' the more confusing emotions started to surface. I suddenly could barely stand to be around Mom. My life felt like it had gone to hell in a hand basket, and it felt like she was half to blame. It was easy to point out Dad's faults, but I used to watch her egg him on many times. She never seemed happy with him, even during the best of times.

As much as she was done, well, I was feeling done too.

It was only a few weeks later when I told Mom that I wasn't coming back to the studio.

Her eyes flew open. "I can't believe you're doing this to me. You're turning out just like your father." She wiped a few tears away with an angry movement of her hand. "If you go, that's it, there's no coming back."

Her tears had the opposite effect on me. I didn't know what she was crying for. My family had been ripped apart, with my brothers running to their friends and me to mine. Nothing was the same any more. I was ready to erupt all over her, but bit my tongue and packed my stuff into a plastic bag. She didn't say anything more when I left.

Life in the loft was very different from my house on the hill. There wasn't a ladder to get up to this loft, but a solid staircase. When I realized it was my place I spent the first few minutes admiring the wood trim and knocking on the walls to feel how solid it was. The loft was completely finished, with drywall and paint. It had a full bathroom. It was the first time I'd lived in a real house since I was a little boy in Wildfire Rim. It kind of made me choked up.

Thomas' parents welcomed me from the beginning. They knew about Dad, but they didn't ask me too much about him. Thomas' mom took me under her wing. She didn't pull any punches, just laid it on the line. "You keep your butt in school and graduate." Another time she said, "I'll kick your butt if you do drugs." She'd also pester me to get good grades and not to skip class. I didn't always do what she asked, but her words stuck with me. It kind of felt good to be looked after.

*****

A few weeks later Thomas and I headed out of Truck Depot at the end of our shift. We rounded the corner, bone tired, talking about the Truck Depot's new waitress, a cute girl from school who was in way over her head dealing with the rough customers at the job.

I spotted a white Toyota truck parked in the front of the lot. In the shadows, a man leaned against its side. My stomach dropped. It was my dad, waiting for me. My legs locked up for a second, before I caught myself and tried to appear cool.

"Hey," I said. I glanced at him from the corner of my eye, making an effort to seem unconcerned.

His hands were jammed into his Carhartt's pockets and he stood up from the truck. His eyes looked relaxed. "Hey, Son. How's it going?"

I didn't know how to answer that, so I gestured to Thomas, "This is Thomas."

My dad shook his hand. Thomas' eyes darted between the two of us, and he gave a half smile.

"Taking care of yourself?" I asked. Dad looked pretty thin and wiry since I'd last seen him. But, the smile was back on his face. I hadn't seen that for a long time.

"Yeah. I got myself a roommate up on the hill. Things are pretty good. You should come up and visit some time."

"Yeah, okay, maybe." I nodded. He opened the door to his truck. I could see a few empty bottles on the floorboards, and a case of beer on the seat.

"Come on up, Son. Maybe we could tip back a few and go throw a fishing line in. The river's been amazing." He slapped me on the shoulder. I stiffened. He lowered his eyes. "See you soon, maybe."

Then a nod to Thomas. "Nice to meet ya."

As he drove away, Thomas said. "He seems cool."

My heart felt like a lead weight. I missed my dad.

Chapter 15

Alice told me I had a phone call. I wiped my wet hands on my dirty apron and picked the phone off the counter. It was Dad. We hadn't talked since he surprised me a few weeks ago. Hearing his voice made me feel awkward.

"Hi Jim."

"Dad, I'm working."

"What time you off?"

"Uhh."

"I'm headed to the river this afternoon to do some fishing. I want you to come."

I rested my forehead against the ceramic tiles on the wall. Rolled it back and forth.

"Yeah, sure. Okay." I said.

"Great. See you later, alligator," he said.

Those words gave me a hitch at the memory. "Yeah, yeah, after a while," I said, and hung up. I started to grin.

Alice brushed past me carrying an enormous bowl of potato salad. "What are you smiling at?" she asked.

I rubbed my mouth. "What? Nothing," I said, and went back to the sink.

Alice's shift ended at the same time mine did. At the time clock, I asked her for a ride, cringing a little because I was sixteen and needed to get a car. Alice never minded giving me rides, calling me a good kid, which kind of made me laugh. She dropped me off a half a mile from the river, and I walked the rest of the way.

Dad was sitting on a battered lawn chair by a bend in the river. He had his shirt off, and a gold chain glittered in the sun around his neck. I shook my head. He must've thought he was something else. Dad had my old fishing pole lying next to him. His fishing line was already in the water, and he watched it with his hat pulled low. Next to him was a six pack of beer.

I walked down the rocky beach, being careful of any ankle busters that might roll lose. He looked up when he heard me. There was a sandy log nearby that had recently been river junk, and I straddled one end and gave him a slight wave. He popped the tab of the beer and leaned over to hand it to me.

I looked at it for a moment, my heart churning inside of me. So many thoughts rushed my head, like cattle charging to get through the gate at the same time. Then a bigger, stronger thought knocked them all down. If you can't beat 'em, join 'em.

I grabbed the can. Dad sat forward and took a beer for himself. He popped the tab off of his, foam running down his hand, and glanced back at me.

My can was wet with beads of condensation. I held it up to my mouth and hesitated, then took a big swig. Dad smiled and tipped back his own.

I knew that by drinking the beer Dad saw me as a man now. And something inside of me rose and grew. I wanted that.

Scooting up, I grabbed my pole and fiddled with some bait, then dropped my line in. We didn't say anything, didn't feel like we needed to. Sitting quiet on that log with the sun beating down on me, no other sounds but the river burbling against the rocks; well, it'd been a while since I felt felt so happy.

He whistled when I reeled in a beautiful speckled trout. Later, I nodded when he pulled in his. We watched the sun turn the horizon all pink and orange, and the air became considerably cooler. Then, Dad pulled in the line, so I stood up to packed the gear. He folded up his chair and carried it by its rusty leg. I followed him to his truck.

"Can I drop you off somewhere?"

"Yeah, Thomas'." My voice cracked from being quiet for so long.

He cycballed me. "What? You moved out?"

"Yeah." I threw the gear into the back of his truck with a clatter.

Dad stared at me for another second, before he climbed in back and dumped his fish out from the bucket into the ice chest. He nudged the fishing poles to one side with his foot.

"Why don't you and Thomas come over Friday? I'm having a few friends up at the house."

I nodded, trying to act nonchalant. Inside the emotions were churning again.

Chapter 16

Friday came. I felt both hot and cold about the party at Dad's that night. My stomach roiled with strange zings and nerves, anxious that I'd somehow mess it up. Or he'd mess it up.

It was the longest day of school ever. Going down the hallway to my third period I saw Brett, my friend from math class, standing at his locker. He always gave me his homework to copy, and in return, I'd share the answers to the tests that I'd get from the kid in the period before us.

Brett waved me over, then slapped me a high five when I stopped. "Hey, how's it going?"

I gave him the thumbs down.

He reached deep into his locker to get behind a thick stack of books. "What've you got going on tonight?" He pulled down a book, and a pile of loose papers spilled out. "Crap!" he muttered, trying to catch them on his leg.

"Party up at my dad's place." I gave a half-smile and shrugged.

He bent down and picked up the papers, cramming them into the bottom of the locker. Then he straightened and slammed the metal door. "Cool." He nodded. No explanation needed about why a dad would party with his kid. He'd heard all about my dad.

"Want to come?" I asked.

Brett shuffled the books in his arms. "Yeah, maybe I'll check it out."

"It'll be fun." I felt better. I could have my own posse there with me for protection. They'd be my shield so I didn't have to feel any weird emotions around Dad. It was going to be pretty strange being at the house again, just for starters.

Word spread. I don't know if it was curiosity about my dad or what, but a whole gang of kids told me they planned on showing up.

I had to work after school, and caught the metro bus to the Truck Depot. Thomas was going to meet me later to pick me up.

It was a crazy day at work. The other dishwasher didn't show up, sick with "Friday partyitis." I busted my butt all evening, trying not to stress about my friends arriving without me at Dad's house. At eight o'clock my shift ended. I closed the dishwasher on the last load of dishes, and glanced around at the clean kitchen, then ran to the time clock and punched out. As I opened the back door, Dean, the new restaurant manager, called me back.

"Hey! Where do you think you're going?" His black eyebrows furrowed at me.

"My shift's over. I'm off."

"They're bringing back another load of dishes. You can't go!"

"Have Margie do them. I'm off the clock!"

"I don't care what you are. You stay here until all those dishes are gone."

The kitchen door swung open, and a trolley loaded with dishes was rolled in by the busser.

"Get to it." Dean said, before walking out to the dining room.

Just steps away, outside the back door, Thomas pulled up. He gave me a grin.

The pile of plates settled on the trolley, sending a couple cups crashing to the bottom of one of the bins.

Thomas honked his horn, and waved, "Come on!"

You want your dishes gone, fine. I'll get them gone.

I pushed the trolley past the sink and over to the trash can, freshly emptied with a clean black hefty bag.

Thomas honked again.

We're late! He pantomimed through the window.

"I'm coming I'm coming." I waved back.

Very carefully, very quietly I lifted out a stack of the thick white plates and put them in the trash. I stacked the second load in. Glass clinked around. I looked over my shoulder, no Dean. I piled in the last of the dishes, and rolled the trash can to the back door

"Dishes are gone," I muttered, and shut the door behind me.

Outside I waved Thomas to come help me. The trash bag looked pretty heavy. Thomas slammed the door, ignoring my finger in front of my mouth. "Shhh dude!"

"What?" he shrugged.

"Help me get this bag into the dumpster."

Thomas arched an eyebrow at me. As we lifted the can the dishes clinked inside. He laughed. "Oh man! What did you do?"

"Hey, I was only doing what he asked!" I said.

We heaved the bag into the dumpster with a loud crash, then I pushed the can against the wall. With a huge grin, I jumped into the GTO. It was Friday night and time to party.

We headed out of town with the music blaring. Ten minutes later, Thomas roared up my old driveway that was lined end to end with cars. Like I suspected, my friends were already there, and Dad had some friends too.

The inside of the house was packed with people. I picked out Dad's friends right away. They all wore the same outfit of muscle tank tops, gold chains, and cut off blue jeans.

Then, I groaned when I saw my friends talking with Dad's people. There were beer cans everywhere. Empty. Tons of laughter. Everyone was feeling good and having fun.

I grabbed a beer and tried to catch up. Dad sat in his battered easy chair and waved his hand at me, "Hi." He didn't wait for my wave back, but returned his attention to a crowd of people, mostly my classmates.

Surreal anxiety shot through me. My friends were partying with my dad without me. What the heck? This was my dad! These are my friends!

The weirdness twisted me all up. I chugged the can of beer trying to shrug it off. Giving a loud burp, I crushed the empty can and got another one. Then, I broke into the crowd around Dad.

"And that!" he yelled, his eyes flashing at the people around him, "is how you clean a hose!"

Everyone around him laughed at the punch line. I'd missed the dirty joke but chuckled anyway. Quick, drink more beer. All this weirdness will go away in a minute.

Many cans later, the music was thumping and all us kids were getting rowdy. We went outside to build a bonfire. Dad was gone. He'd left at some point with a couple of his friends, maybe to get more beer, or headed to the bar. I didn't care. I was whooping it up and having a good time.

I drank until I puked. I don't remember how Thomas and I got home that night, but the next morning I woke up in my bed still fully dressed. Even my shoes were on. The phone was ringing, feeling like it was imbedded somewhere inside my brain. Slowly, I sat up, holding my head to keep things still. After a couple of seconds of not moving, I leaned over for the phone.

"h..Hello?"

"Son?" Dad's voice boomed, hail and hearty.

"Yeah?"

"Where the hell is the middle cushion for my couch?"

"What?"

"My couch! My cushion!"

"It's missing?" My brain puttered. I had no idea. I could barely remember last night.

"Hell yes, it's missing!" He grumbled a little, before he gave a laugh. "You sure know how to party, Son."

Chapter 17

It'd been a little more than a year since I moved in with Thomas, and I was seventeen now. Every weekend was a party at Dad's place.

The alarmed buzzed, forcing me to wake up. I blearily glared at the alarm clock before pulling the pillow over my head to muffle the sound. It might have worked too, if Thomas hadn't been pounding on the door. "Just want to sleep!" I yelled the last word, at Thomas or at the alarm clock, I didn't know.

Earlier this morning, I crawled into bed smelling of stale bonfire and cigarettes. I'd hoped to catch a few hours of sleep before staggering off to school. Soon I wouldn't be worrying about school anymore. I was graduating in a week.

More pounding on the door. "Just break it down, why don't you?" It was a weak demand, I never kept it locked.

Thomas burst in, his curly hair flying in every direction. "Dude, c'mon! We're late!"

I rolled out of bed and slowly stood up. After rubbing my eyes I inspected the clothes I had on. Pants three days worn without being washed. I grabbed the front of my t-shirt and took a sniff. Gah! Beer, and who knows what else.

Thomas thumped down the steps. "I'm not waiting for you, dude!"

I rifled through the dirty pile on the floor looking for a t-shirt less grimy than the others. Finding one that would do, I yanked it over my head and stumbled down the stairs. School, blech.

At least I'd get to see my brother, a freshman at the high school. I hardly ever saw him anymore. I didn't go too often to Mom's house because she always gave me a hard time. She knew I was living kind of rough. Whenever I saw her she'd shake her head and say, "You're just like your dad." I didn't want to hurt her and give her the response I wanted to say, so I avoided her.

Her nagging at me made me feel like I could relate with Dad. I understood him better because of what Mom thought of me.

Besides, I liked the way I lived.

Or so I told myself. Somewhere along the way a tiny voice told me I'd compromised, and I started to feel scummy inside.

But, alcohol always beat down the scummy feeling.

I jumped in the car just as Thomas rolled down the driveway.

"We hanging with your dad tonight?" he shifted the car into second.

"Yep!"

"Cool." Thomas stepped on the gas and we flew to school.

*****

That night, Dad was waiting on the front steps of his house when Thomas and I roared up the driveway. Thomas slammed the car to a stop and I jumped out. Dad stood up with his truck keys dangling from his finger.

"C'mon kid, let's get trucking." The pun caught him, and he slapped his knee with laughter.

I grabbed the Toyota's side-wall and checked the back of his truck. Dad had plenty of beer back there.

Dad sauntered over, thumping his sneakers as though they were cowboy boots. "I want to go down to the trestle for a bit."

"How long you been drinking tonight?" I asked, although I already knew the answer. His breath was so fumy I'd be nervous to light a match near him.

"Never too early to start, Son!"

"Five o'clock somewhere, right Dad?"

He laughed. "Screw five o'clock."

I climbed in to the driver's seat of the Toyota. Thomas drove his GTO up next the passenger side and rolled down his window.

Dad paused in mid-swing up into the seat, shouting to Thomas. "We're going to the trestle." He reached into the back of the truck for a beer, before scrambling the rest of the way in the cab. He slumped into the passenger seat with a groan and popped the tab.

I stepped on the gas and roared down the driveway, making him gag at the sudden rush of beer into his mouth. He sputtered, "Damn, watch my truck, Son!"

I smiled, threw it into second gear and squealed out onto the main road. Black smoked followed me as Thomas squealed his tires back.

But, we didn't get out of town for another forty-five minutes, because Dad made me run him through the drive-thru to get super-sized fries. After that, we had to gas up. It was full-on dark by the time we arrived at the turn around under the trestle.

Arriving at the dead-end, I pulled the e-brake and did a little fish tail. The truck came to a stop, and Dad climbed out, stumbling a little as his foot caught the ground.

He took one look around. "Crap. Can't see nothing." He climbed up on the tire to reach the cooler and got another beer.

It's true, another cloudy night meant no moon. Thomas' GTO rumbled up next to us. "We gonna stay?"

"Hell no," Dad said. "You boys brought me here too late."

Thomas grinned. "Let's go do some donuts down behind Truck Depot."

"You wanna do that, Dad?" I asked. I couldn't see his face in the dark, just his shadow as he shrugged.

"Why the hell not," he said, taking a swallow. He climbed back in and slammed the truck door shut.

I clicked on the radio and flipped through the channels, then circled to pull back on the road. Those thrills of excitement were growing in my stomach. I'd never taken Dad's truck spinning before and I gripped the steering wheel hard in anticipation. Dad was quiet, probably focused on drinking.

Clearing my throat, I started to tell him about some engine work Thomas and I had done on his GTO. Dad didn't say anything in response, but I saw the bottle tip up. I zipped the truck neatly around a bend, just as Dad opened the door to throw the empty beer bottle out. The door snapped shut as I came out of the curve.

"So Thomas's planning to go to Spokane to get some tie rod ends for the GTO," I said. "I'm going with him. We'll be gone a few days." I down-shifted as another turn approached. "Trying to be back by Monday, because we're supposed to be moving. We got an apartment with a couple friends." No response. I cleared my throat. "What are you doing Monday? Maybe you can help us move?"

I bumped off the road and into the dirt parking lot behind Truck Depot. As the truck coasted under the streetlight I twisted towards Dad.

He wasn't there.

Empty seat.

My heart skipped a beat. I let the truck idle for a minute, trying to wrap my mind around what happened. Then I threw it into gear and slammed on the gas back the way I came. Adrenaline shot through my veins with the explosion of ten cups of coffee, just imagining him lying flat someplace like road kill.

I came back around the bend to a car stopped in the on-coming lane. My heart sped faster.

It was Thomas' GTO. His car's headlights lit up a man sitting cross-legged in the middle of the road. I pulled up alongside. Dad looked up at me and slurred, "I think you dropped something."

"What the heck did you do?" I asked, shaking. He got up and brushed himself off.

Thomas hollered out his window, "I nearly ran him over! He was just lying there!"

Dad climbed back in the truck and began in an exasperated tone. "I can't believe you just dumped me out. And left me! Left your ol'man."

Inside me, the shaking had changed. It started deep in my stomach and I started to swerve. Laughter burst out of me, until tears streamed down my face.

*****

The following Monday, Dad let me borrow his truck to load all of our crap for the move into the new apartment. We didn't have much in the way of furniture; some old car seats for the living room, and mattresses on the floor. But we had plenty of alcohol and space to have our own parties.

We had the best parties, but all that drinking eventually did catch up with me. One afternoon, after a late night, I woke up to another phone call.

"Jim!"

"Dad?"

"Hell no, this isn't your Dad. This is Jared. Your boss. You're late again."

Oh Crap! I sat up in bed and looked for the clock.

He continued. "Don't bother coming in today. You're fired."

Rent was due, and it wasn't looking good.

I came home the next afternoon to a pretty girl sitting on the kitchen counter. "This is Joe's friend," Thomas said. "She's looking for a place to stay."

Just like that we had money for rent, and a new roommate.

Chapter 18

The new girl slid off the counter and stood leaning back on her hands. She had on some of the tightest blue jeans I'd ever seen.

"Hi, I'm CeeCee."

Wow! She was a looker. Blonde hair, curves in all the right places. Play it cool, I told myself, cracking open the fridge for a soda.

"Hey, I'm Jim," I answered back.

I grabbed the soda and tried to lean against the fridge nonchalantly. The fridge moved under my weight, making me spill the soda down the front of myself. Inside I cringed, while flicking off the droplets like nothing happened.

The front door slammed opened, and Dad was there.

"We going out, boys?" he asked Thomas and me.

Thomas grabbed his hat off the counter and pulled it over his curly mop. "I'm in," he said.

"Hell yes!" I said, setting the can down. Then, as if it weren't a big deal, I told the new girl, "You hungry? Help yourself to anything in the fridge." Her eyes got big, blue… gorgeous. She gave me a huge smile that melted my heart.

"Uh, yeah, see you soon," I stuttered before kicking myself out of the house.

"Who's the girl?" Dad asked as we headed for the truck.

"New roommate," I muttered.

Dad looked over at me and laughed.

*****

CeeCee was a talker. I tried like heck to be aloof around her, but she just had a way of worming herself in that made me feel awful chatty every time she was near. She gave me bits and pieces of her back-story on how she came to be living on her own at seventeen. It sort of made me want to take her under my wing even more.

The next week I was hired on at a landscaping company. It wasn't much, but I couldn't really mess up mowing, and the boss liked me okay. CeeCee worked at the little restaurant downtown. I started to meet her there to walk her home when her shift had finished.

On this night, I think I got a mite too close when we were walking, because out of the blue, she told me she wasn't interested in dating anyone. "My life is kind of crazy," she laughed, "I can barely take care of myself, let alone anyone else."

I doubted that.

"I don't mind crazy." I gave her a small smile. She flashed me a grin and did a little skip on the sidewalk.

We stayed up all that night talking. At three a.m., and then again at four, I told her, "C'mon, let's call it a night."

Both times she said, "Okay, after this last cigarette." And so here we were, throats sore from smoking, watching the sky turn grey until the sun peeped up over the window sill. I gave a big yawn, and she turned to me with a sweet smile. "You poor baby. Having to work with no sleep. You're amazing!"

I had to smile back. She made me feel amazing.

It was close to our second week of late night conversations that I rolled a little closer to her. Reaching out with my finger, I brushed a strand of hair off of her cheek. She didn't pull away. I studied her eyes, wide and blue. I leaned in and kissed her.

Best kiss of my life.

"Be my girl," I whispered.

Her smile about melted my heart when she whispered back yes.

*****

About two weeks later, we both had the weekend off from work, so I took her down to the river to the place where Dad and I had fished. I parked the car, a beat up Pinto, off the side of the road. Her door was up against the bushes, so I grabbed her hand and helped her crawl over the gear shifter and out my side.

"This is nice!" she said, looking up at the thickly surrounding trees that grew right up to the shore of the river. I pulled a knapsack out from the back seat and then slammed the door.

"Yeah, I like it here." I smiled at her, popping the trunk.

She walked back to me to take the fishing poles as I lifted them out. Reaching back in, I yanked out the metal tackle box and banged the hatch shut.

"Okay babe, let's go!" I led the way down a tiny path just barely visible in between the bushes. It opened up after we got through the trees.

When it widened, she pushed past me and skipped ahead, walking across the bigger boulders with her arms flung out to keep balance.

It made me smile. In front of us was the same old log that I'd sat on while fishing with Dad what felt like a hundred years ago. She ran right over to it and claimed a spot of her own, the same place where I had sat, and set the poles at her feet. With a flip of her hair, she turned to look at me and patted the spot next to her.

"Come sit here, hon." And, flashed me that smile. Man, she made me feel things I'd never felt before; smart, confident, unstoppable. I started to smile back.

Then, I stumbled, and the tackle box corner caught me sharply under the knee cap, grinding me to a stop. There was no sucking up the pain. I grimaced and hobbled to the log in halting steps, like a chicken chasing a grasshopper.

"Are you okay?" she asked, shielding her eyes from the sun with her hand. I dropped the fishing gear and bag and sat next to her.

"Yeah," I laughed. "Just kind of klutzy." I examined my knee (crap, not even a cool war wound) and gave it a rub. "Want a beer first? It might be warm."

She wrinkled her nose at the thought of warm beer and shrugged. "Okay."

Reaching down, I unzipped the duffle bag and pulled out two cans. I handed one to her and put the other by my feet. My can didn't want to sit nice on the rocks, tipping over as soon as I set it down.

I sighed, and flipped open the tackle box. "Let's get your pole set up."

She scooted closer to me when I started baiting her hook. Mmm, she smelled like vanilla. She tried to take the pole after I'd finished, her hand just above mine, but I hung on to it to tease her.

"Give me!" she laughed. I leaned in and gave her a slow kiss. For a minute everything fell away.

"I love you," I murmured against her lips. The kiss ended. She pulled away and wouldn't meet my eyes.

"Umm," I studied her. "Did you hear me?"

She took the pole from me and stood up. After a few practice flicks she cast it into the water, the line catching a glint of the sun as it stretched across the water.

"You know I can't say that back." She sighed. "I like you. I like you a lot." She didn't turn to face me but continued to stare out at the river.

I popped my beer and took a long gulp. Yep, warm.

After baiting my hook, I cast the line into the water and settled onto the log. CeeCee crouched back on her feet where she was.

"Come sit here," I said. She shook her head. We sat in silence for a few minutes.

"Want me to make a fire?" I asked, trying to break the awkwardness.

She jumped at the idea. "Yes!" Then, with a wink, "We'll need it since I'm about to catch dinner."

"What? No way!" I argued back.

"I've got a good feeling," she teased back, taking a sip of her beer. She frowned and quickly set it down.

Great. I was batting 0-2 now.

Glancing around, I found a couple good sized rocks and propped my fishing pole up until it was secure. After that, I walked up the beach gathering an armload of driftwood.

Once back at my pole, I reeled it in a few spins. Still no bites. I figured I had to be falling rapidly from amazing, to unremarkable in her eyes after this.

CeeCee was sitting on a big river rock and held her pole like it was a sword. What a goof, I smiled, and started to build the fire.

"Oh my gosh!" she shrieked. "The pole is moving!"

Sure enough, the tip of her pole was bobbing up and down.

"I think I have something!"

"Pull back! Yank it hard!" I yelled, dumping the wood to one side.

Her brows wrinkled as she pulled and reeled. I stood behind her like a backseat driver, with my hands jerking in the air, wanting to reel it in for her. The fish came out of the water with its tail whipping. I let out a holler.

"That's a beaut!"

She swung it up to the shore where it flopped like a silver eel among the rocks.

"Oh get it! Get it!" she squealed.

He was a slippery sucker, and it took me a second to nab him. "Come here, you!" I muttered. Finally, I had the hook free from its mouth, and held it up like a fat trophy. "Dinner."

She frowned. "Oh, the poor thing. Put him back."

The fish wriggled in my hand, its mouth opening wide and white. "You want me to release it?"

"Yes, let him go." She pushed her bottom lip out. "I'll make you a dinner instead. Whatever you want."

I walked to the river's edge and let the fish slip through my fingers back into the water. We watched it swim away. She came over and leaned her head against my shoulder.

"In that case, I like steak," I said, and gave her a squeeze.

Chapter 19

I did try my hand at being romantic. One night, on the way to meet her after work, I picked a few stems of flowers that grew in a shrub by the Shop Rite. The flowers were bushy with layers of pink petals, and smelled like her perfume. I thought she'd love them. As I admired them, I noticed hundreds of black specks that filled the center, wiggling in the petals. They were covered in bugs.

Crap!

I shook the flowers as hard as I could, petals and bugs flying everywhere. Suddenly, I wasn't too sure about my gift, but she had already seen me and was running down the steps of the restaurant.

"Jim! How beautiful!"

I felt a little dubious as I held the flowers out to her, my fingers and toes all crossed that I'd shaken them clean.

"I love them!" She plucked a flower out and moved it to her blonde hair to pin it behind her ear.

"Maybe you should, mmm" I swallowed, "smell them first."

She held them to her face to take a sniff, and then froze. From her look I knew there were still a few more critters squirming in there. She looked up at me with wide eyes, not sure of what to do. I laughed, "It's okay, you can toss them." Like a baseball player, she pitched them through the trees. Then she took my hand.

She made me laugh like no one had. We had a good time together. She understood me. She thought I was important, and I wanted to be that for her.

There were times when CeeCee could get awful down though, when the mood struck her. It was a major point of contention when I'd tell her that I loved her. She'd shake her head and push me away.

It had been getting worse lately. "You're just going to leave me," she cried a few nights ago. I was flabbergasted. No matter what I said I couldn't change her mind.

My insides felt tight with worry when I saw her withdraw from me more and more, for no reason that I could see. I felt pissed at her mom and dad that she didn't believe that anyone could love her. I didn't know how to fix what was happening between us.

Tonight, it started again. We'd ordered pizza and just brought it home. I hadn't finished my first slice when she said, "I know this isn't going to work." Her eyes puddled up, and she grabbed her napkin under the plate of pizza.

"What?"

"This," She indicated her hand between me and her.

"Aww babe, it's definitely going to work!" I leaned over to give her a hug, and she pushed me away.

"What?" I asked.

"You don't understand."

"Then tell me."

She sniffed and gave me a small smile. "I'm okay. I'll figure this out."

Standing up, she squeezed my shoulder and then went into the bathroom. She wasn't in there but a minute, when, out of the blue, cold fear grabbed my heart. Call it a premonition; I don't know what it was. I jumped up and pounded on the door.

"CeeCee! You okay?" I yelled, my ear pressed against the door listening. The fear inside me was so strong I couldn't grasp the crazy thing I was doing.

"I'm fine!" Her voice sounded too cheery after our last words.

Urgency seized me, smothering all rational explanations.

"CeeCee!" I rattled the door knob. "Open this door."

"Jim! I'll be out in a minute. Let me use the bathroom in peace, sheesh." She gave a laugh.

I knew her, I knew her laugh. Something wasn't right.

I called one more time. "You either open this door, or I'm breaking it down."

"Oh my gosh, Jim, just give me a second please!" Her voice had panic in it.

I started to kick the door before the words were fully out of her mouth. The door was flimsy, two kicks and I had it down. I burst into the room.

She was sitting on the floor. There was blood everywhere. A bloody razor sat on the counter.

My heart froze inside of me.

"What did you do?" I whispered.

Her eyes looked like two pools of shame. In her hand was a wad of toilet paper, smears of blood across the floor in front of her from where she tried to wipe it clean.

I rushed over and drew her up. She couldn't meet my eyes.

"Where did you hurt yourself," I murmured, turning her arms over to look for cuts. I found them on her ankles. Six deep slices that pooled blood around her feet.

"Why?"

She started sobbing, deep throaty cries, and buried her face into her hands.

I scooped her up and carried her to her bed. The lump in my throat wouldn't go away. I grabbed a wash cloth, and wiped my eyes with it before getting it wet with cold water.

She still sat on the bed, and stared wet eyed at me, stunned at my return.

"Oh babe, poor thing." Seeing her precious feet covered in blood broke me. I started to cry as I tried to stop the bleeding. "Please. Please don't ever do this again."

That seemed to break her. "I won't! I'm so sorry!" she cried, her lips in the crown of my hair. "I hurt so badly inside thinking of you leaving. I know I'm not good enough to keep you. You are the best thing that's ever happened to me. I'm so sorry."

"You're more than good enough. You're more than good enough for me."

I got the bleeding to stop, and bandaged them with some gauze I'd found under the sink.

Then, I cleaned up the bathroom. When I came back to the room she was lying down wrapped in a blanket. I lay next to her and held her. "I love you hon. I'll never leave you. Never. You're my treasure. I love you forever."

She buried her face into my shoulder and whispered, "I was always too scared to tell you before, but I love you too."

*****

It was three weeks later that I asked CeeCee to marry me. She shrieked, "Yes!" And, about knocked me down trying to kiss me. We were poor as could be, so I drew a diamond ring on her finger with a marker. "One day, this will be real," I promised her. She climbed into my lap, and with a wink, said, "I'll make you a steak that night."

The next Saturday, I took her to the house on the hill to officially introduce her to Dad. When we pulled up to the garage-house I noticed it looked really run down. He hadn't held a job in a while, and I knew where his spare money went.

We went inside, and I was surprised to see that the interior was neat. Dad was in his recliner watching the A-Team. He looked up as we walked over to him. His brown eyes looked a little glassy, and my step faltered a bit. I cleared my throat and then said, "Hey Dad, meet my future wife, CeeCee."

He grabbed her hand, and she peeped over at me nervously. He gave a belch, and said, "Congratulations, Son. You got a looker." CeeCee smiled and tried to pull her hand away. Dad wasn't letting go. Too late, I realized he was deep in his cups.

"Sit down, why don'tcha? Have a drink with me." I reached across and pulled her hand away.

"Naw, we got to get going."

"Aww, c'mon. Stay awhile." He smiled at CeeCee. She pressed back against me.

"Another time, Dad."

On the way back to our apartment I felt something in my gut. Seeing Dad sitting there, all alone, after a life time of going from job to job, hit me like a knife blade of grief and determination all in one. Mom had always said I was just like my dad, but, for the first time, I wanted to be someone different.

I just wasn't sure how.

Chapter 20

It was cloudy on the day I got married. We didn't have a lot of support for our marriage. Mom and I were kind of on the outs; Dad didn't care about weddings. Her parents were not in the picture. So here we were, ready to stumble through our vows in the office of a Justice of the Peace.

CeeCee reached for my hand for reassurance. I gave her a wink and tried to look confident, but inside I was a mess of butterflies and jitters.

"Do you want the long version or the short version?" the JP asked and tapped his pen on the document before him.

"Uhh," I stammered.

The JP looked up at the ceiling and sighed. "The long version is where I talk about God. The short version I'll pronounce you both married."

The word, "God" pulled at me. "Long." I nodded, then pulled CeeCee closer.

The JP shook his head. "You're standing on the wrong side of her," he muttered.

"Oh!" Already, I was doing this married thing wrong. We quickly changed places.

He opened a black book and began the ceremony. Her ring was from the drug store, mine was her class ring that barely fit past my first knuckle. He pronounced us man and wife. To be honest, we could have gone with the short version, because those were the only words I heard. I kissed her and joy exploded inside of me. I finally had my own family.

One I didn't want to screw up.

The only way I knew how was to go back to my roots. I used to talk to God as a kid, and I figured now would be a good time to start up again.

We could have gotten married at our church, but we'd only been going there for a few weeks. CeeCee was a brand new Christian, and I was barely one myself.

We drove home from the courthouse, stopping first at the gas station where CeeCee found me a metal band ring in a display on the counter while paying for the gas. I carried her through the doorway of our new place, a tiny studio apartment above a video store. It was as plain as could be, but already furnished with a bed in the corner and a battered bookcase. Pushed against the far wall was a card table with three flimsy chairs. We felt rich.

As soon as I set her down CeeCee scampered straight over to the bookcase. She ran her hands along the top, then spun towards me with her eyes sparkling.

"I'm going to paint this, and fill it to bursting with books! As many as I can find!"

I had to laugh. To be so excited over a bookcase, she really must love to read.

The next day I was back to my landscaping job. As I pushed the lawn mower, my silver ring caught my eye. Wow, I'm a married man. I have a wife. I couldn't get over how surreal it felt.

After work, I opened the front door and yelled out, "Honey, I'm home. Hope I can find you in this mansion!"

CeeCee was curled up on the bed with a book. The studio felt cozy. I looked about to see what had changed in the apartment. Candles were lit. She'd found a tablecloth from somewhere, covered the chairs with matching towels, and had dinner cooking on the stove.

She gave me a big kiss that I was happy to return.

"Mmm smells good!" I growled into her neck.

"Get in the shower and clean up!" she giggled.

Dinner that night was a little unexpected. Spaghetti, with sauce made from tomato soup. I poked at the noodles with a fork, lifting them to look for the sauce.

"I'm sorry!" She blushed. "I thought you were supposed to use soup." She gave me a sad smile, "I've never really cooked in a kitchen before."

I took a big bite. "Delicious!"

"I promise I'm not trying to poison you." She grinned and handed me the salt and pepper. "Maybe this will help."

*****

A year later, soon after we turned twenty, we had our first baby, a girl. My daughter was beautiful, fragile, scary. When the nurse handed her to me my arms felt wobbly, like I was holding fifteen eggs all at once. I cradled her as carefully as I could, scared that I would break her somehow. My wife watched me from the hospital bed with a content smile, her face still flushed and sweaty from the difficult delivery.

My family. The responsibility pulled at my core. Joy and fear rushed through me, tearing me in different directions.

Later that night I went outside for a cigarette. I looked up at the stars and prayed. Oh God, don't let me fail them.

The hospital released the both of them a few days later. I fought with the car seat for ten minutes while the nurse watched and CeeCee giggled. Finally, she eased herself out of the wheel chair, and said, "Here, let me try." After the baby was buckled in, I gave her a shaky smile, and we all went home.

Right away I discovered that parenting wasn't easy. Our daughter had colic. From the time I came home from work, until two in the morning she screamed. After a few weeks, my wife was frazzled, the baby was hurting, bills mounting up, and there was no one to turn to. Now, we were the grown-ups.

The frustration at not being able to fix what was wrong was eating me away, and after another night of only three hours of sleep I had to escape. It was the first time that I felt so out of control since Dad had been arrested when I was fourteen.

I needed a drink.

That Friday night I brought my wife and my daughter to Dad's house. He'd moved in with his girlfriend, and the atmosphere at his new house was less rambunctious. We laid the baby down on the bed in the bedroom. CeeCee coupled her hands under her chin and watched our daughter, asleep now earlier than she'd ever had before.

"She'll be fine. We'll check on her." I whispered in CeeCee's ear. She nodded and followed me out into the living room.

Dad had the bottles opened for us when we walked in.

"Having a hard time?" he asked.

"Yeah." I collapsed back on the couch like a dead weight, and felt like it was the first time I was able to relax since our daughter had been born.

"Just keep looking up, Son."

"I'll drink to that!" I held up the beer. Over the next couple of hours I drank a few beers and laughed; only stopping when I knew I had to sober up so I could drive.

There was a nagging feeling inside of me that I shouldn't be doing it. But I squashed it down pretty quick.

After a month of going to Dad's every weekend I started thinking about alcohol every day during work. I couldn't wait until Friday, and the closer we got to the weekend, the more the hunger grew. It started to seem silly to wait a whole week for Friday to come so we could unwind. Maybe we'd stop by his house this Wednesday. CeeCee agreed.

We buckled the baby in the car seat like every other time. I smiled at CeeCee. Her eyes were shining in the dark. Aww, I thought to myself. I'm glad I'm giving her a break. It isn't easy being stuck in the house all day with a crying baby.

I put the key in the ignition and twisted. The car wheezed, but refused to start. Frowning, I tried again. The starter whined over and over, nothing.

"What the heck?" The car had been running fine all week.

I tried it again. This time the radio died out, and the headlights dimmed.

CeeCee shifted in her seat. This was getting a little more serious. There wasn't any money in the budget to fix the car, or even miss a day from work because of lack of transportation.

I tried it again. No lights now, in fact the ignition switch refused to even click.

I tried it again, and again. Nothing.

We sat there in the dark. I rubbed my hand down my forehead as I realized the car was broke-down. At the very least it needed a battery. Even that expense we couldn't afford.

CeeCee nervously twisted in her seat, and the seatbelt pulled tight across her chest. "Honey?"

I took a deep breath and held it for a second, then prayed out loud for the first time. "God, I need this car for work tomorrow. If this is your way of telling us to quit going to my Dad's to drink, please let this car start." My hand was sweaty from gripping the key so hard.

I put it in the ignition again.

Held my breath and turned it.

The car roared to life, headlights and radio blaring.

CeeCee scrambled out and twirled to stare wild-eyed. "Oh My Gosh! Never again, Jim!"

I slowly flipped off the ignition, numb. CeeCee was shaking as she unstrapped the baby. She clutched her close as we headed up the stairs to the studio.

Once inside, I shut the heavy door and bolted it, then wandered numbly to the couch. I sank down to sit with my head in my hands. What just happened? Was I becoming hooked on alcohol?

Was it too late?

CeeCee went to the walk-in closet and laid the baby down in the crib. I could hear her singing to our daughter, some silly song about a bird in a gumdrop tree. Her voice, soft and lilting, calmed me too.

The hunger inside me groaned, but I shoved it down. Like a light bulb going off, I finally realized how to be different than my dad.

I'd never drink again.

Chapter 21

CeeCee and I were in our tiny Mazda on our way home from grocery shopping. Thinking of all those bags of food in the trunk made me feel like a good provider.

"Aren't you the cutest peanut?" CeeCee had turned around from the passenger seat to hold our daughter's out-stretched hand. After months of suffering, colic had finally released its hold, leaving a happy baby girl. My heart welled up with joy at the very thought of her.

My attention was caught by a staggering hitchhiker up ahead. He wore shabby clothes, and his jeans were ripped up one leg, but it was his jacket that made my heart pound. A worn-out denim Carhartt.

It was Dad.

I swerved to the side of the road, making CeeCee squeal. Dad's face lit up and he ran to the car, nearly toppling over at the door when his momentum carried him too far.

He looked at CeeCee in the front seat and waved, before wrenching open the back door and plopping into the seat.

CeeCee's eyes opened wide as the alcohol fumes filled the air.

"Why hello little mugwump," Dad said to my baby. He reached for one of her socked toes to wiggle it.

I eased back into traffic. "Where you going, Dad?" I glanced in the rear view mirror at him.

His facial features froze. "Who you calling Dad?" he snapped. No smile now, instead, he had an aggressive curl to his lips.

The hair on the back of my neck prickled. "Uh, it's me, Jim."

"Jim who?" Dad squirmed and grabbed for the door handle.

I licked my lips and glanced over at CeeCee. She studied her hands in her lap as if staying still would keep her from being noticed.

"Dad! It's me! Your son, Jim."

He grabbed on to the back of my seat and pulled himself between CeeCee and I. He looked at me closely, the stench of stale cigarettes filling the air, then settled back.

"Let me out," he mumbled.

"Dad, where you going? Let me take you?"

"Let me out now!" he yelled.

CeeCee nodded, "Let him out if he wants to go."

Inside, I cursed. What was I supposed to do? Let him out on the road where could get hit by the next car?

"All right, hang on," I said. There was a fast food restaurant a few blocks away.

Dad started to push on my seat, rocking it back and forth. "I want out now!"

I yanked the steering wheel and turned into the parking lot. He wrenched the door open and toppled out. He didn't look back as he stumbled away.

The next afternoon, I called to check on him. Dad wouldn't take my phone calls. He must've remembered how he hadn't recognized me and felt embarrassed.

That moment marked a permanent change in our relationship. Coming at the heels of me quitting drinking was too much for him to deal with. Dad already felt abandoned by me because I went to church. Although he believed in God, he saw that as an act of betrayal that I'd join forces with "those people". The people he felt judged by, the people he wasn't good enough for. People like my mom.

Although I'd tried to reassure him many times, there was nothing I could say that would change his mind. He couldn't see that I loved him just as he was, even if, and especially if I didn't live the same lifestyle.

After a few months passed, I ran into him at the grocery store as he stood in the bakery picking through the pecan pies. "Well, hey! Long time no see." He smiled, and slapped me on the back. We stood there for a few minutes catching up, and he had a new story about wrangling with a collection agency that he shared with a chuckle.

But, he didn't seek me out any more, and when I called to see if he could go fishing he was always too busy. If I wanted to see him then it was up to me to make it happen. And I tried, I hunted him down and went to wherever he was, trying to rekindle our relationship.

He didn't reciprocate.

He had assembled his own tribe, made up of college kids who lived next door and guys from the bar. They lived the same lifestyle. They were the ones who made him feel safe and valued.

It hurt, but at the same time made me angry that he couldn't receive that from me.

One night I called him, after I'd found out he'd driven past my house to go target practicing with his new tribe.

"Dad, how come you'll go shooting with the kids next door, but don't have time to go hunting with me?"

"Jim, those boys, they're my sons."

The air around me went cold. "Whatever, Dad." I snarled the last word, and hung up. Red haze pushed down the lump in my throat. I grabbed a cup off of the counter and flung it against the wall where it shattered into pieces.

Chapter 22

A few more years went by. We had four children now, and I loved them more than I knew I was capable of loving. They were amazing.

I took them fishing with me down at the lake. My three year old daughter caught her first fish, and I'd hardly gotten hers off the hook when one of my sons hauled one up. Then my other daughter . I was running back and forth so much taking care of their lines that I didn't have time to throw my line in. It was a great day, even though the baby did get into the fishing bait.

But, the responsibility of sports, bills, family, and my job wore on me. I still didn't drink, but, I didn't know where else to turn for relief. My brothers had their own lives, and we all scattered to different corners of the state. I checked up on them as best as I could by phone, and we made an effort to get together once or twice a year over at Mom's house. They had great families, and I was proud of them.

Mom and I still had a tense relationship. She did her best as a mother, but now she never seemed happy with who I was as her son, nor how I was as a father to my kids. But, I loved her a lot despite the difficult times.

Dad and I had a tentative truce, although we still didn't talk all that much. I'd pretty much given up on having a relationship with him.

CeeCee was the love of my life and my best friend. Still, as anyone can tell you, marriage is a lot of work. But we worked hard at it, and I was a happy man.

And then life throws you a curve ball.

The phone rang.

It was Dad on the other end. It had been months since I'd last talked to him, and the first time he'd called me in years.

"Hey, Dad!" Even after all we'd been through, I felt excited to hear his voice.

"Hey, Son."

Instantly my blood went cold. I could hear it in just those two words. Don't say anything more. I don't want to know.

"I need you three boys to come to my place this weekend." He coughed. "I've got something I have to tell you."

My brain screamed, "Tell him you're busy!"

"Wh...what Dad."

There was a heavy silence. I heard Dad take a deep breath, and it gave way to a hitching sigh. He took another, and then another, while I waited, holding the phone so tight it shook against my head.

"It's not good. The Doc says your Old Man's got pancreatic cancer."

The words were like a gut punch. The air ripped out of me as I grabbed on to the wall for support. I couldn't think of how to respond to him. Every thought was a rush of cuss words and shock.

"Uh, okay. Okay Dad. I'll be there on Saturday." Somehow I got through the rest of the conversation and hung up the phone. I sank to the couch with my head in my hands.

CeeCee came from the kitchen where she'd been folding laundry.

"Are you okay, hon?" She laid her hand on my shoulder.

I ripped my hands through my hair and stood up.

"NO! I'm sure as Hell not okay!" I wanted to throw something. I grabbed a pillow off the couch and threw it back for being so stupid and soft. I wanted to destroy something. Tear it into a million pieces, like how I felt inside.

I stormed outside to the garage, flung open the door and stood for a moment in the dark gloom. My heart pounded. I grabbed the edge of the work bench to steady myself, then squeezed it as hard as I could. Dad's sick. I felt like was fourteen again, realizing I was going to be left alone without a Dad.

A sudden stab of agony ripped through me and I clung to the bench for support. It was the death of a hope I'd carried since I was a boy, that one day he'd quit drinking, one day he'd want to be around me.

It was never going to happen.

I grabbed the chainsaw off the bench and threw it. Now I was forced to make amends with a man who didn't give a hoot about me or my family.

I rubbed my face in my hands and struggled to push the emotions down. Don't feel, don't care about this man who doesn't care about me. He only wants me now for God knows why, to drag me through the same crappy feelings that he was feeling.

Angry tears filled my eyes. "Dammit," I muttered, and wiped them with the back of my arm. The wetness infuriated me even more, and I punched the workbench. I hadn't cried since the birth of my daughter.

The front door slammed, and there was a crunch of footsteps on the gravel coming up the path outside. A second later, CeeCee stood silhouetted in the doorframe watching me.

I looked up at her with my eyes burning.

"We'll get through this," she said softly.

I grabbed my splitting maul. "He made his bed, let him lie in it," I said, as I pushed passed her to the wood pile.

*****

The next day I came home from work convinced that I was going to skip the visit up to Dad's place on Saturday. CeeCee had dinner for the kids already on the table. After I came out of the shower, she said, "Get dressed. We're going out."

We went to the local diner, just one step above a truck stop in niceties. I slid across from her in the vinyl bench of the booth. Her eyes wrinkled with worry, and I could tell she had something to say.

The waitress came to our table and took our orders. After she walked away, CeeCee started to fiddle with the sugar packets.

"What? Spit it out," I said.

She took my hand and looked me in the eye.

"Babe, I know this sucks. I know you are feeling a storm inside. But you have to listen to me. The time will come for you to be able to deal with all you feel. But right now you have to go to your dad."

I yanked my hand away. "I'm sick of it! He did this to himself! How many times did we tell him to quit drinking?"

"I know, hon."

"Remember two years ago when he almost died, because he had withdrawals so bad?"

"He was trying to quit."

"Cold turkey! He almost killed himself! Only to start right back up again."

"I know honey, I know."

"He couldn't put that damn bottle down, and now he's sick and dying." I grabbed the butter knife and dug its edge into the table. "I'm so mad at him. What does he want from me? Sympathy? After all the years of abuse, anger, punching things, and scaring us? Cutting me off and making me feel like crap because I didn't drink with him?" My eyes started to blur. "Now he calls to tell me he's dying, and for what? So I feel sorry for him? He deserves this! He stole from me, made me fatherless." I grabbed her hand again, and she looked scared. "I have a son. I know what it's like to bond with your son. I got ripped off. I don't ever want to speak to him again." My words choked off. I couldn't speak over the lump in my throat.

My wife stroked the back of my hand. "I know baby, I know sweetheart." She picked up my hand to kiss it. "I'm so sorry."

The waitress set down a burger in front of me. It was as appetizing as a pile of dirt. I couldn't eat it. "Just pack it up to go," I said.

*****

That Saturday I did go up there. Willie, David, and I sat crowded together on his couch in his crappy living room in a run-down trailer park he'd found himself in. We were silent as we listened to his diagnosis. There wasn't a lot to say. But seeing him, so vulnerable and afraid, curled up in his old easy chair made it easy to squash down all the anger and try to be there for him.

I went every weekend after that for over a year. Dad couldn't drink through the vomiting from the cancer treatments. His once muscular frame whittled down to almost nothing through the months, and that broke my heart. But, it was the first time since I was a boy that I looked into his clear eyes.

We didn't have any deep heart to heart talks. No matter how he looked on the outside, he was still a tough old bird at his core. We talked about sports, hunting, and his drinking buddies' latest adventures. He joked about how he'd played the "C" card when the collection agencies called to make them feel bad. He tried to stay active, even canning his famous pickles. He gave me a few jars, and I ignored the mold that grew in them because he was going blind.

We had one important conversation. It was about six months after his diagnosis, and I'd called Dad to check on him. We small-talked like usual, but burning in my heart throughout the conversation was something I wanted to say, needed to say. Something I'd been avoiding.

I cleared my throat. "Dad, I just want you to know that I love you." There was absolute silence on the other end. Men did not talk about love to one another. There was more I wanted to say. I took a deep breath, and the words came in a rush. "I want you to know that I don't blame you anymore. I know you did the best you could when I was growing up. I know that your marriage wasn't easy. I know you had an addiction. But you're a good man, you always have been. I love you, Dad."

There was a sigh on the other end of the phone. Dad said, "Yeah, well it is what it is." He changed the subject to his garden and how proud he was of his carrot crop. My guts squeezed inside. I felt the blockage of his shame. It was like I was speaking a foreign language, and he couldn't understand me.

CeeCee walked in as I hung up the phone.

"He didn't get it," I said, feeling a different grief rip through me.

She put her arms around my shoulders and gave me a soft hug. "I love you."

I realized then she loved me despite my weaknesses, loved me truly for me. And for some reason, I understood in that instant that what made me different from my dad wasn't quitting alcohol, it was facing my emotions and not hiding from them behind anger.

"I had this picture while you were talking to your dad," she continued, speaking quietly in my ear. "It was of your dad and Jesus up in heaven. Jesus turned to him and said, 'Remember when your son told you that he loved you?' Then Jesus explained to him what you meant. It's going to work out. He'll understand one day. I'm proud of you, babe."

I knew anything was possible, but I had my doubts.

*****

It was on a Tuesday when I got the phone call saying we needed to go to the hospital. Dad was having a procedure to help drain some fluid off of his lungs, and time was short. I was numb with fear, I knew the day was quickly coming when I'd have to say goodbye. I'd seen the events play out in my nightmares.

Going home after work to get my wife and kids, and then leaving for the hospital was the longest drive of my life. But, I wanted to take my time, go as slow as possible, because I was afraid of the outcome.

We pulled into the parking garage. My wife and kids all climbed out of the mini-van and we headed for the entrance. Trying to corral our four kids through the hospital hallways and into the elevator already wore me out.

When we walked into the room, Dad was lying back in bed. He sluggishly lifted his hand like it weighed a hundred pounds. "H..hey." His words were garbled.

My stomach clenched. There was an obvious degrading in his health since last week.

He rolled his head across the pillow to look me in the eye. "I'm sorry," It came out a whisper. I rapidly moved over to him and leaned down.

He exhaled; it hissed out like a punctured tire. "I really want to stick around, but I can't. I'm going to have to go." He could barely get the words out. Fear and sadness flooded his eyes.

I rested my forehead against his shoulder, determined to be strong for him. "I'm here, Dad. I'm not leaving."

My kids rallied on all sides of the hospital bed, my youngest son barely tall enough to peep over the blankets. Dad slowly turned his head, and then when that became too much of an effort, moved his eyes to look at them all. They were a little wide-eyed at all the beeps, medical tubes, and wires attached to Grandpa, but they settled into comfortableness pretty darn quick. My baby daughter found a black comb on the side table and started to comb his thin hair. Her sweetness made me smile because she didn't know him very well. He'd lost those opportunities, gone forever now.

He closed his eyes, maybe enjoying the feel of the comb being pulled softly through his hair.

"Dad," I said, resting my hand on his shoulder. He opened his eyes and grabbed me with his intense look. I swallowed, then pulled my ipod from my pocket. I unwound the ear buds and carefully put one in his ear. Climbing down on my knees, I leaned next to him and put the other ear bud in my ear. Then I pushed play.

It was a song by Mercy Me, "Word of God Speak." A faint grin crept across his face.

When it was over he whispered, "Play it again, Son." So I did.

He was so skimpy and thin, with no meat on his bones, but his hand had swelled to almost normal size. There was gauze on his arms, and the skin was weeping. It broke my heart. Softly, I cupped my hand around his. It had been a long time since I'd held my dad's hand. The memory hit, almost overwhelming me, of holding his hand as a little boy. We were in the river, and I was scared to cross because the rocks were so big. Dad had looked at me and said, "I think we can make it, Son. Here, take my hand." His hand had been so big and strong, rough from all the hours of working outside. I felt safe. When I slipped on the rocks his strength held me up.

Now I held his to comfort him until he was across the other side. I wasn't going to let go until he went from life into death into life again. I wanted to make him feel safe, but there was nothing I could do to help him.

His other hand crept across the blanket, until it bumped into my wife's. He tried to move her hand, but was too weak, so she lifted his. He set her hand tenderly on mine, then rested his on the top of both.

"Good." His word was breathless. I knew what he was saying. He was saying stay together, no matter what, work it out. I held back my tears.

He began to breath shallower and shallower. I started holding my breath too, trying to control the scream that was growing inside of me.

Breath

Ten seconds later.

Breath

Twenty seconds.

Breath

Thirty seconds.

I bent down close to his mouth to see if I could feel air come out or if his chest was moving. There was nothing, just a blank stare.

On the other side of the room, a voice said, "Someone get the nurse."

Two nurses came in. One gently pulled me away and hugged me. The other nurse checked with her stethoscope, slowly going across his chest. After a minute, she straightened up, and looking at the floor, she shook her head. "I'm sorry. He has passed on."

Then, the nurse stated the time of death.

Crushing pain tore through me. I yanked away from the hugging arms and slapped the wall behind me in fury. That's it? I wanted something, anything. I'd heard the stories of death beds, I was waiting for some sign that he was okay.

He was gone, and I didn't notice anything.

I turned from facing the wall to look at Dad again. He was staring at the corner of the room. Walking over, I tried to close his eyes, but they wouldn't stay shut.

Even that infuriated me.

Grabbing the handrail I breathed deeply and glanced at my family, still gathered around the bed. I didn't know what to do next. I looked back at Dad.

I didn't want to leave him.

Suddenly, Dad tipped his head up.

He got a really big smile on his face.

Every hair on my body stood, electrified.

The nurse sucked in her breath.

Dad's eyes open wide like he saw someone he was thrilled to see just come into the room. Then his eyes narrowed as though staring into a bright light. He squinted real tight like he was trying to see what was behind the light.

Then, like an exhale, he relaxed. His head drooped down, and I knew then my dad was gone.

We were all stunned, I think. We backed away from the bed, and nurses scurried out.

The next day I called the nurse, because I'd heard people sometimes move after they die. She said, "What happened to your dad after he passed will impact me for the rest of my life."

*****

I wish I could tell you things all wrapped up nicely with a bow. That, emotionally I felt healed because my dad smiled after he died, and all the parts of me that felt ripped off went away. It didn't work like that.

Grieving sucks.

It's hard and painful. It ebbs and flows. One minute I felt like I had a handle on it, the next I was filled with surreal shock; "My Dad's gone!" as if it just happened that very second. "I'm never going to see him again!"

At least not in this life.

The funeral was horrible and good all mixed together. I hated that I was there. I was thankful for the support of our family and friends and appreciative of the stories shared.

He was a man who loved his family. Loved his boys, his brother, and his sisters, and was proud of them. He'd be the first there when there was a house flooding or pipes froze up.

But, addiction chained his life. It robbed him of what he could have been, and that's why we were truly grieving. But even in that place, we could see who he really was, a man who had the best sense of humor, was strong, and would give a stranger the shirt off his back. We grieved over the chains, over the loss of unrealized relationships and potential.

I wish he had lived long enough to understand that I truly loved him. That, despite everything we'd been through, he was, and always had been my hero. It was my last crushing blow that he'd only heard my words through a filter of shame, and had rather push me away then deal with his own guilt.

I felt like I would fly apart from the grief.

But life goes on. In the meantime, I looked over at my wife, the two of us once broken and now making a family together. Both of us had grown up learning a wrong definition of love; earn it because you're not worthy. Now learning everyone has value. Both of us changing, and trying to teach our kids love, so they could be loving people.

She smiled back at me and reached for my hand. "You know," she whispered. "You are just like your dad. All the best, strongest parts of him live in you."

I had no words to answer her, no way to describe the gift she gave me. She had given me the gift of finally being able to feel proud that I was like him.

I felt like I could breathe in deeply for the first time.

And slowly I picked up the pieces.

Chapter 23- Epilogue

This next part of the story is going to be hard to believe. You've traveled this far with me, and I appreciate it. I just have to warn you, I don't have any explanations, theological or otherwise, for what I'm about to tell you. I can only share it the way that it happened to me.

Okay, here it goes.

It was about ten o'clock in the evening. My wife was in the living room talking with our oldest daughter. All the other kids were in bed. I got up to get myself a drink of water, and then meandered to the back to bed.

On the way there I heard my son calling to me from his bedroom.

"Dad! Dad! Come here!"

I went into his room and flipped on the light.

"What's up, Bud?"

He was lying on his back on the floor with his eyes closed, and a huge grin on his face. He was crying, and had been for a while, with wet tracks down either side of his face soaking his hair. I paused in the doorway, kind of taking it all in. Then, I sank to my knees next to him.

"What's going on, Son?" I rested my hand on his arm.

He said, "I see him!"

I froze, and all of my hair stood on end.

"You see who?" I asked.

"I can see Jesus! And I see Grandpa!"

My boy had a look of joy on his face that I didn't recognize. He was so caught up in what he was seeing, he didn't seem to notice me at all, apart from those few words.

I swallowed then and slowly backed away. Leaning out into the hallway, I called, "CeeCee! Hurry up! Get in here!"

She and my daughter came running at the panic in my voice. They crowded into the room, bumping into one another in an abrupt stop with the same reaction that I had; what in the world was going on?

I really didn't know what to do at this point, so I sat back down, and kind of off the cuff, I said, "Well, tell Grandpa, "hi," from me."

It kind of made me giggle just to say it.

My young son, still with his eyes closed, says, "Grandpa's smiling and he's waving to you, Dad. He looks so young!"

Suddenly there was a lump the size of Pittsburgh in my throat. My eyes started to water.

My wife sat down in the doorway, bowed her head and prayed silently in her head. She told me later that she'd prayed these exact words, "God, please give Jim a special gift with his dad."

All I know is that just then my son opened his eyes and said, "Dad, God has a special gift for you. Grandpa's next to you right this second, and he's saying to you, "I understand how much you love me. But now I love you, Son, more than you'll ever know."

My son had never been privy to the conversation of when I'd tried to explain to my Dad that I loved him, because he was at a friend's house at the time. He had no idea what he was saying to me.

But I knew. Here's my dad telling me the situation's reversed; he loves me with a depth that now I can't understand.

I broke.

God was giving me the experience of agape love and restoration, and what a father's heart looks like.

My kids, CeeCee, and I squashed together in that little room and thanked God. All of us were filled with a deep peace and joy. That night was a special night, one none of us will forget.

I don't know why it happened. Later, my son said that he'd been praying before bedtime, telling God he was sorry for the things he'd done wrong and asking God to forgive him. My son said that as soon as he'd said that he felt a surge of love fill him to overflowing, and then he saw just what I described.

My son is fully confident that his Grandpa is happy, strong, and knows love.

*****

Look up, Son.

Thank you for reading **Lost No More**, the second in the **Ghost No More** series. On the following page is a sample of **Ghost No More, book one,** that I hope you will enjoy. ☺

If you'd like to hear when the next sequel releases, please join the mailing list here: http://eepurl.com/QYxXD

I love to hear from my readers. Here are some more ways to reach me:

http//joyfullivingpafterchildabuse.blogspot.com/

email- ceeceejames777@gmail.com

Facebook- https://www.facebook.com/ghostnomore

Ghost No More

Chapter One

~Turning Invisible~

"You know, CeeCee," Mama said, not looking up at me, "I was lost in the desert once."

I froze, afraid to move a muscle. I didn't want to break the spell causing Mama to talk to me. They were her first words to me in two days.

Mama sat on the floor staring at a picture in her lap-- a picture that Grandma had painted of Arizona. She lit a cigarette, paused to take a deep drag, her eyes focused on the yellow painting.

"Your dad and I were in the Sonoran desert looking for peyote when I was pregnant with you. And then the car died. I told your Dad that car was a pile of crap, but he never listened to me." She snorted and shook her head.

"He had this great idea to take a short cut back to town. Instead, we were lost for hours. I thought we'd die out there."

She jerked her head up and gave me a sharp look, and my eleven-year-old heart jumped. "Somehow, we found our way back. I remember thinking I was never going to get away from him, because of you. I ended up going into labor, and your dad left me alone at the hospital on his way to the bar to get drunk."

She stood to put the painting back in the box.

"Mama, were you happy? You know, when I was born." I blurted out before she could turn her back, and the moment was gone forever.

"You were a terrible baby, just screamed all day. But I didn't let you manipulate me with your crying. I used to let you scream until your face turned black. I kept the bedroom door closed and let your dad deal with you when he got home."

She paused from folding the tissue paper around the painting and turned with a dark sneer. "Don't think he's a good guy. Your dad destroyed your baby book one night when he was drunk."

She abruptly left the room, returning a minute later with a white photo album that she set before me on the kitchen counter. I looked at her for a second and then opened the book. The first picture captured Mama in 1973. She was twenty, beautiful, and smiling with the confidence of a woman who once had every football player at her high school chase after her. I was perched on her lap, and Mama's hands were tucked under her legs to avoid touching me. Another picture caught her in mid-laugh. She was with Dad and his older cousin, her arm coquettishly wrapped around the cousin.

The next page had photos of me as a toddler proudly being displayed in front of my grandparents' fruit trees, flowers, and their house, and in each picture I was wearing a variation of plaid pants and a long sleeve shirt.

"Why am I wearing long sleeves in the summer?" I asked.

"To hide the bruises. Your dad wore so many rings. Your Grandpa threatened to call CPS on him all the time."

I hesitated for a moment, before tapping on the picture of my second birthday. "Why do I have a black eye?"

"Oh, I popped you one that morning because you were being smart to me. Now go outside."

I had an assignment at school the next week to bring in baby pictures. I cut some out of a magazine and pasted those to my project instead.

***

When I was two, my parents and I lived in a farmhouse in Pennsylvania. The house was big and white, with a muddy yard in front, and two garages that jutted out on the side where Dad ran his motorcycle business.

Nearly every morning, as soon as I finished my breakfast that Dad set out for me, I ran outside. He was already out there, working on one bike or another. I was scared to be in the farmhouse alone. The house was hollow and cold; and the wooden floor gave sharp creaks that made my skin prickle. Mama stayed in one of the rooms upstairs. I knew better than to go look for her.

Outside, I sang, "la, la, la, la," and used my shovel to fill my blue plastic wheelbarrow with dirt. I had made a path in the golden grass that led between the two garages. I thought for the most part that life was silent, ants were silent, grass was silent, and my parents were silent. The only sound was my own voice.

There was always a parade of motorcycles lined up in the sun, waiting for Dad to fix them. I pushed my wheelbarrow past them and dumped the dirt at the end, jumping up and down on it to pound the dirt flat. I looked at the motorcycles and squinted. The chrome trim flashed back the reflection of the sun and hurt my eyes. Near one of the bike tires was a pile of gasoline-soaked rags. I loved the smell of gas and crouched over them to smell them. Dad yelled from the garage, "Get away from there!"

Dad saw me! As fast as I could, I ran from the rags into the muddy yard, almost tripping on the rope that tied our dog, Bo, to a rotting dog house. He looked at me with sad eyes. I put my arms around him, my face burying in the fur of his dirty neck and squeezed him tight. He made a quick snarl and bit my arm. I shoved him away with a scream, hurt and anger pumping through my lungs. Mama came out onto the porch with her cigarette and poked it in my direction, "Serves you right for messing with him."

It was the first time I saw her since the night before.

Mama liked to be left alone. Whenever I caught her eye in the house, she'd point her finger to the front door, "Out."

She was also rough if she had to touch me. My stomach felt like I had swallowed rocks if I heard her come down the hall in the morning to help me dress for the day. She'd whip the pants out of the drawer with a dark look on her face and jam my legs into the holes. Then she'd lift me up by the band of the pants and shake me until I slid into them like a pillow in a pillow case. I learned to suck in my stomach because she snapped them quick, more than once catching my skin.

After she pulled the shirt over my head, I'd scramble to get my own arms through the sleeve holes. I didn't like having her hands under my shirt with her sharp nails, where there was grabbing and twisting to get my hands through the sleeves.

Mama didn't like to be around Dad either. One night, I was woken up by a loud cry that came from downstairs. A minute later there was a scream that was abruptly cut off. The hair on the back of my neck stood up as I rolled out of bed. I tip-toed out of my room because the plastic bottoms of my pajama feet scratched on the wood floor. With my blanket wrapped around my arm, I snuck part way down the stairs to peek through the railing.

It was bright in the kitchen. Dad was walking around Mama who sat at the table. His eyes glared with anger, but she wouldn't look at him. He slapped the table next to her, and both she and I jumped at the sound. When he walked behind her, she whimpered, and his lips curled in a snarl. He slapped her with a crack that made me yelp, but I was drowned out by her scream.

I stuffed my blanket in my mouth and curled down on the step. I didn't know adults hit each other; I thought they only hit children. When Mama quit crying, I peeked out one more time and then crept back up the stairs to my room. I squished my eyes tight, trying to stop the image from replaying in the darkness.

It wasn't long after that night when Dad caught me sneaking a piece of candy from my Easter basket. He raised his hand. I flinched and stumbled back. I was afraid of the big ring on Dad's left hand. The blue stone in it winked evilly at me. But, he pointed toward the dark, wood-paneled corner. He had me stand there while he leaned back in a chair and watched me like a cat watches a mouse. With a singsong tone, he directed me, "Stand up. Sit down. Stand up. Sit down. Stand up. Sit down." He sipped from his coffee cup and ate my candy while he watched my legs shake. It lasted for hours, until he grew bored and my candy was gone. My nose slid up and down a black groove in the paneling, and I wished there was an escape.

My third birthday was a few days later. Dad called me to get on his bike. He strapped the white helmet on to my head, and thumped the top twice, "There you go, mushroom head." He grinned and picked me up, setting me on the black seat, and then climbed on in front of me. Mom rode behind me. My arms weren't able to reach around Dad, so I clutched the stiff leather of his jacket at his sides, and my hands ached from the effort. I cried every time I rode behind him, afraid I might let go and fall off onto the rushing blurred pavement. Mama always said, "I'm just waiting for your laces to be eaten up by that engine!"

We roared up to Grandma's house. Dad climbed off, leaving me to scramble down on my own. He walked into Grandma's house before us. Mama pulled me back with a jerk on my arm and said, "Don't you embarrass me. I'll give you a smack you won't forget," before she shoved me into the house. The kitchen was filled with my relatives. I winked back tears. Grandma clapped, and I ran over to hug her knees.

There was cheering so I tried to smile back. My cousins batted balloons back and forth over my head. I watched them and thought the balloons floated by magic.

Grandma gave me a plastic tea-set with a big red ribbon. I felt a splat as my cousin stuck the bow to the top of my head, which made me laugh, until the tape pulled my hair when I tried to yank it off. Someone opened the tea-set package for me, and I set the cups on the tiny plates around the table. Humming, I poured a cup with my plastic teapot. My cousin grabbed at the teapot.

"It's mine! Grandma gave it to me!" I said.

Mama pinched me hard on the underside of my arm and hissed under her breath, "You share that toy with your cousin."

I handed the teapot over to my cousin with a lump in my throat. Mama thought I wasn't a nice girl, like my cousin Christy. "Smile!" There was a flash as Grandma took a picture.

Later, I went outside to have a few minutes by myself. My first prayer came as I walked around on the top of an old railroad tie that edged the garden. My three-year-old self reached out to the Creator, and I prayed over and over in a chant, "Please God, let me start over. Let me start my life over. I will be good this time. I will do it right. I will be a good girl. I will be good."

Available free with Kindle Unlimited

http://www.amazon.com/Ghost-No-More-CeeCee-James-ebook/dp/B00IJ0AKRQ/ref=sr_1_1?ie=UTF8&qid=1406664481&sr=8-1&keywords=Ghost+no+more

Made in the USA
Monee, IL
27 September 2021